AF601956

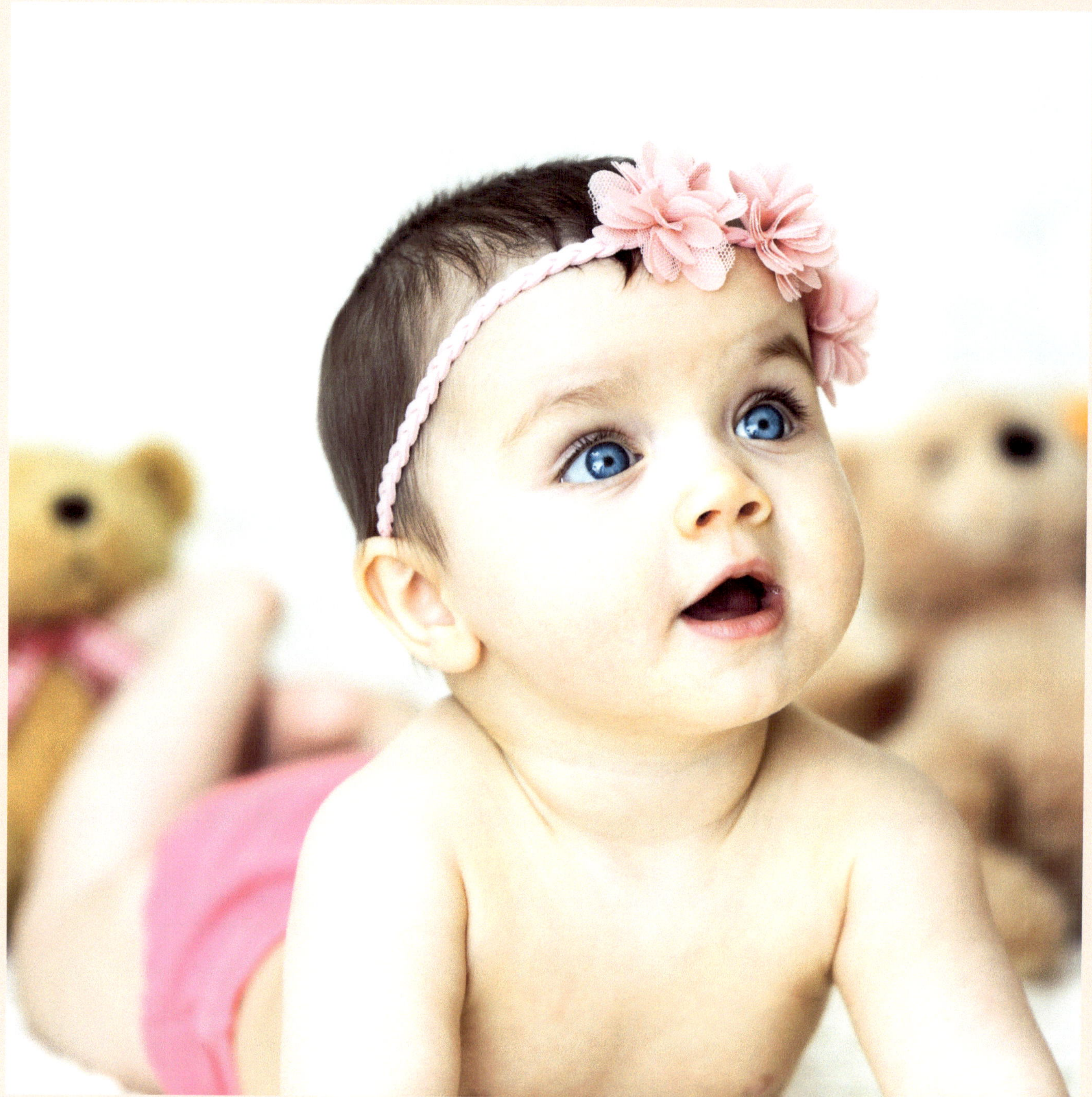

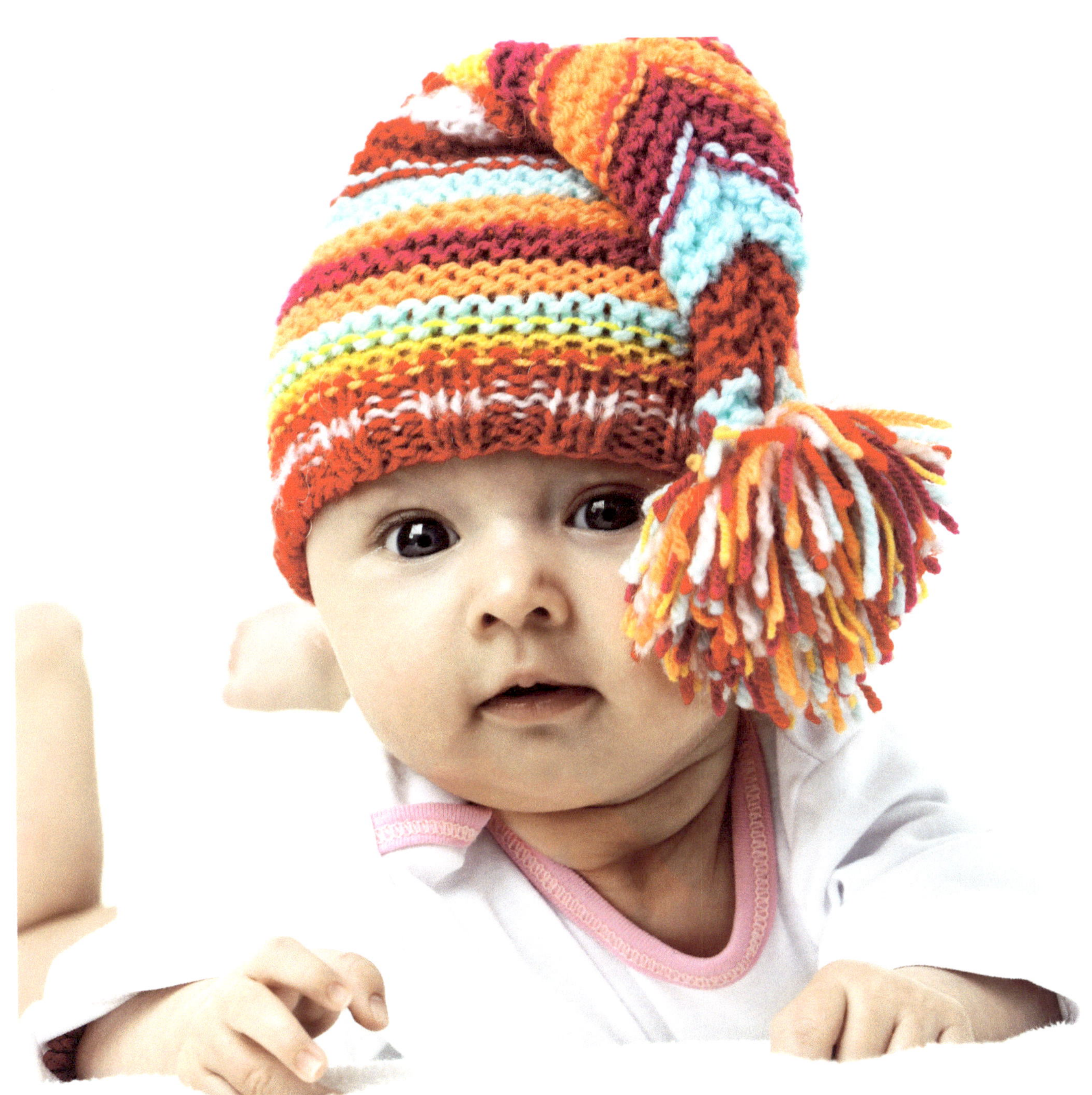

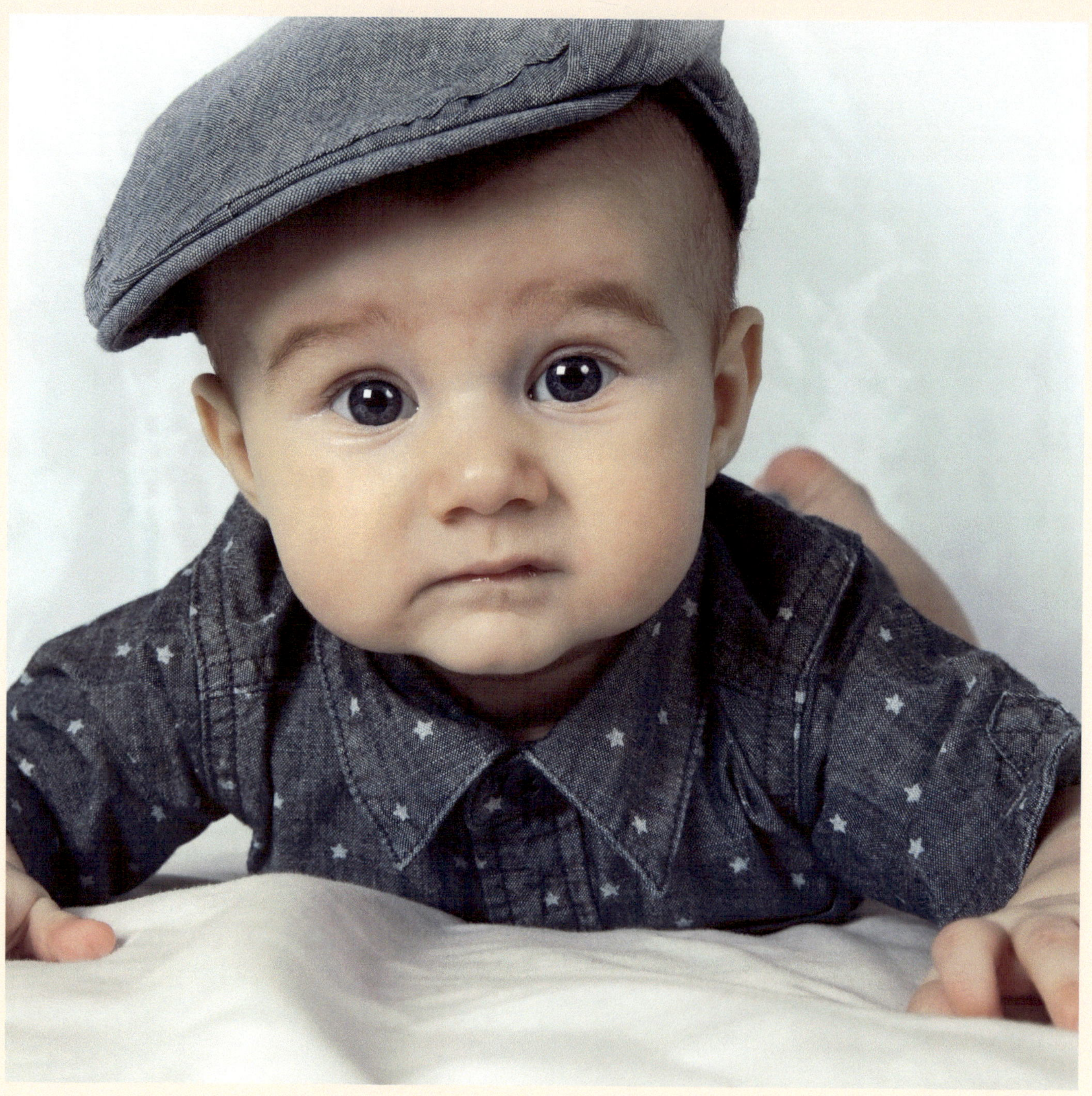

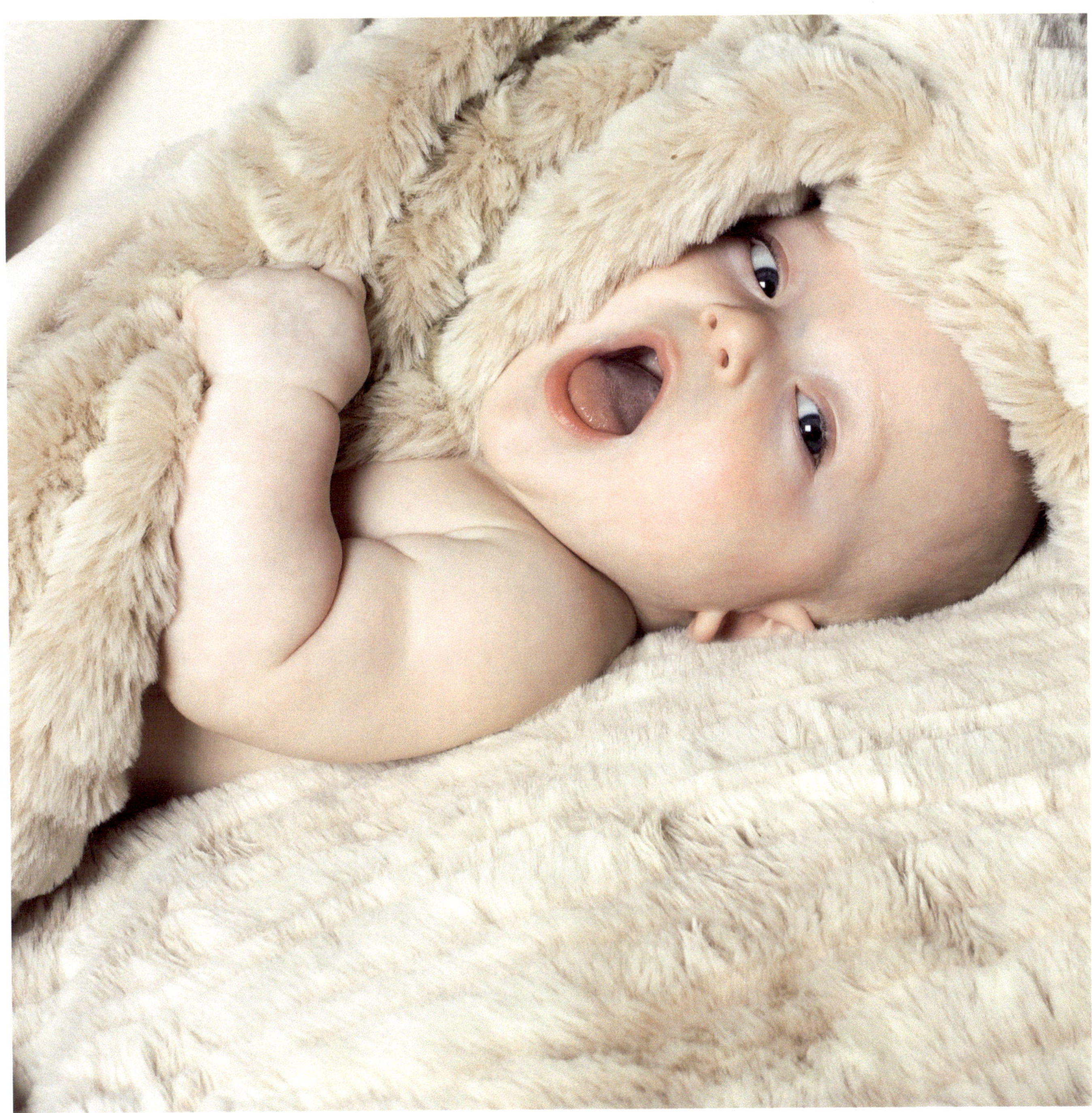

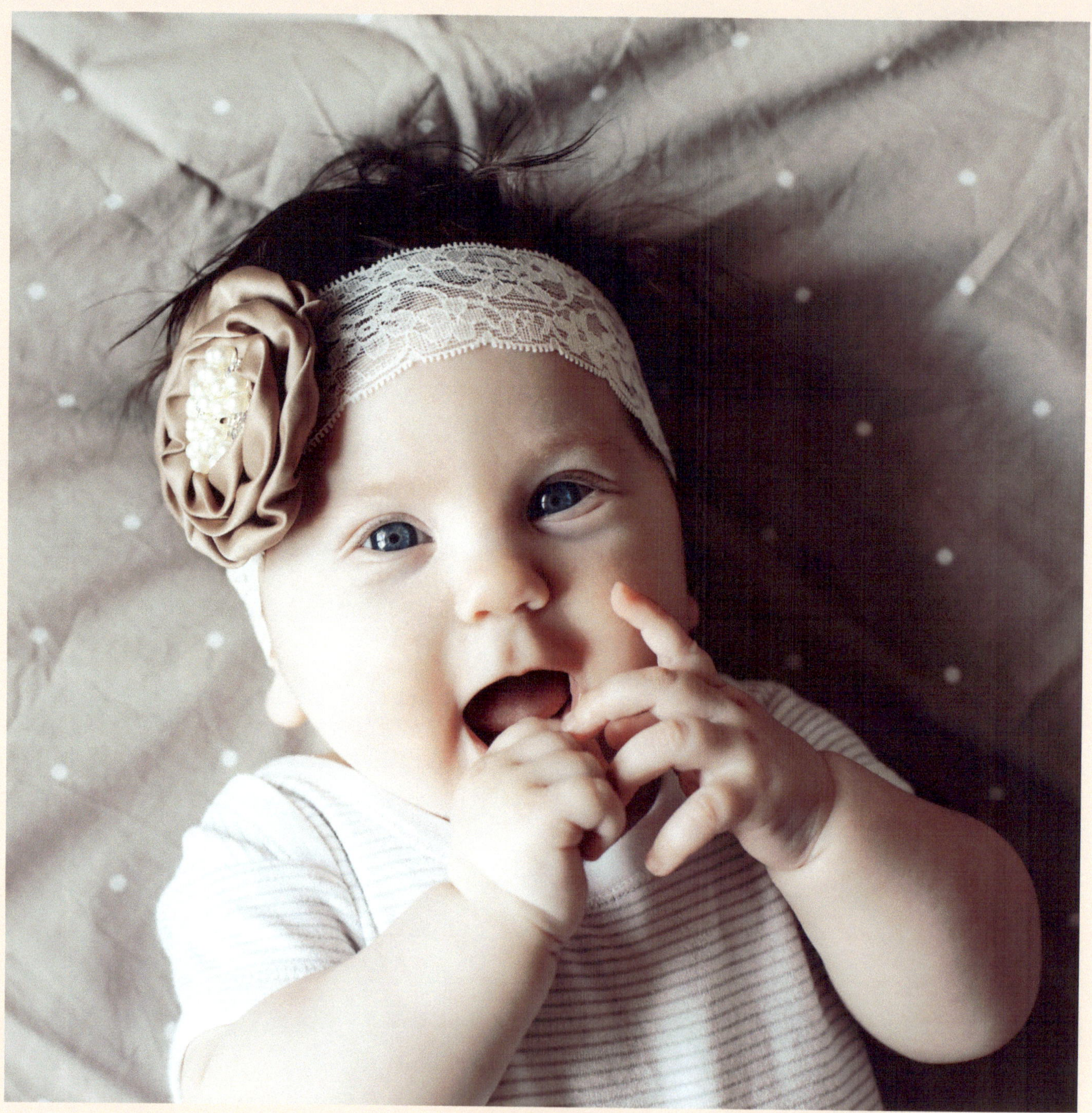

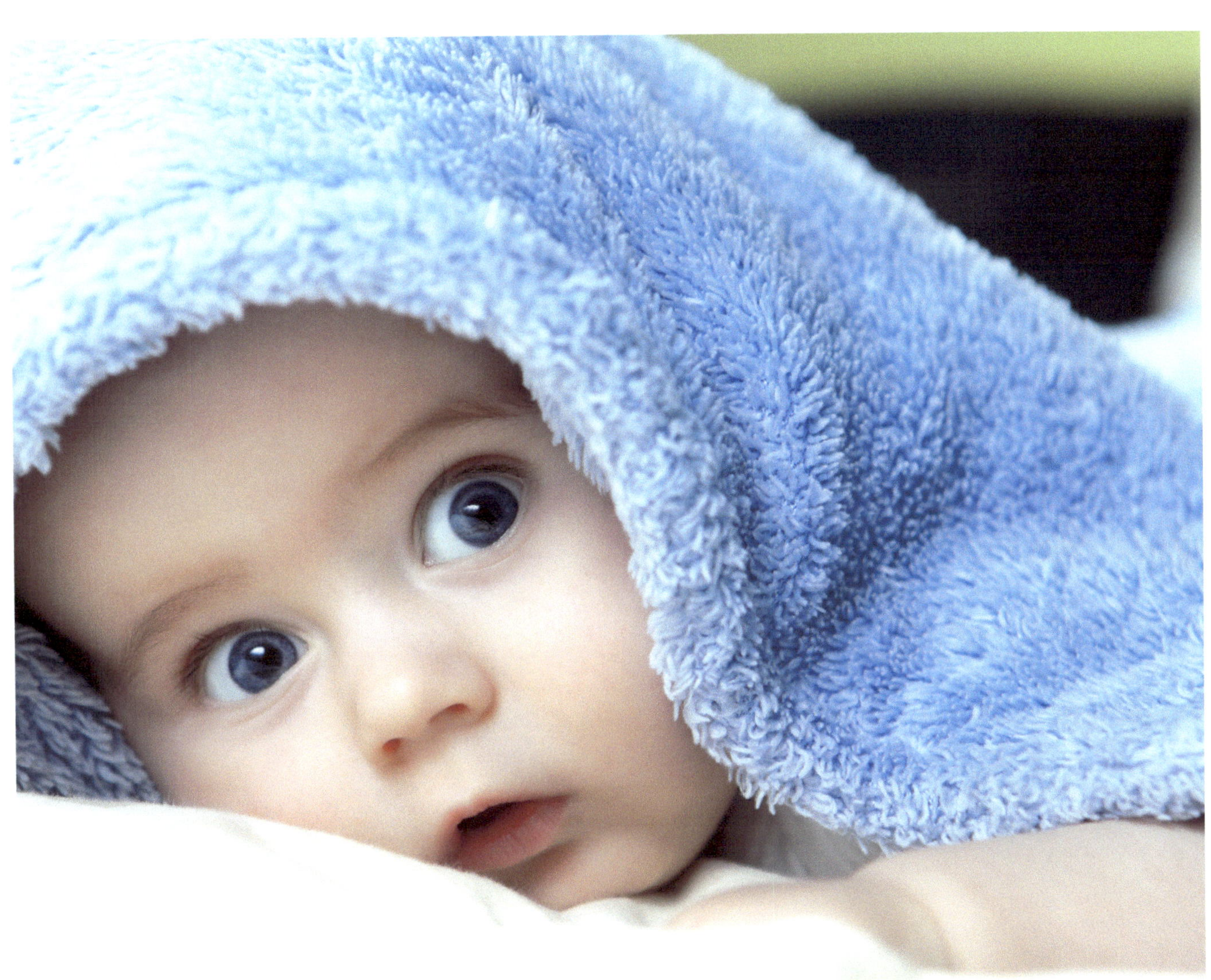

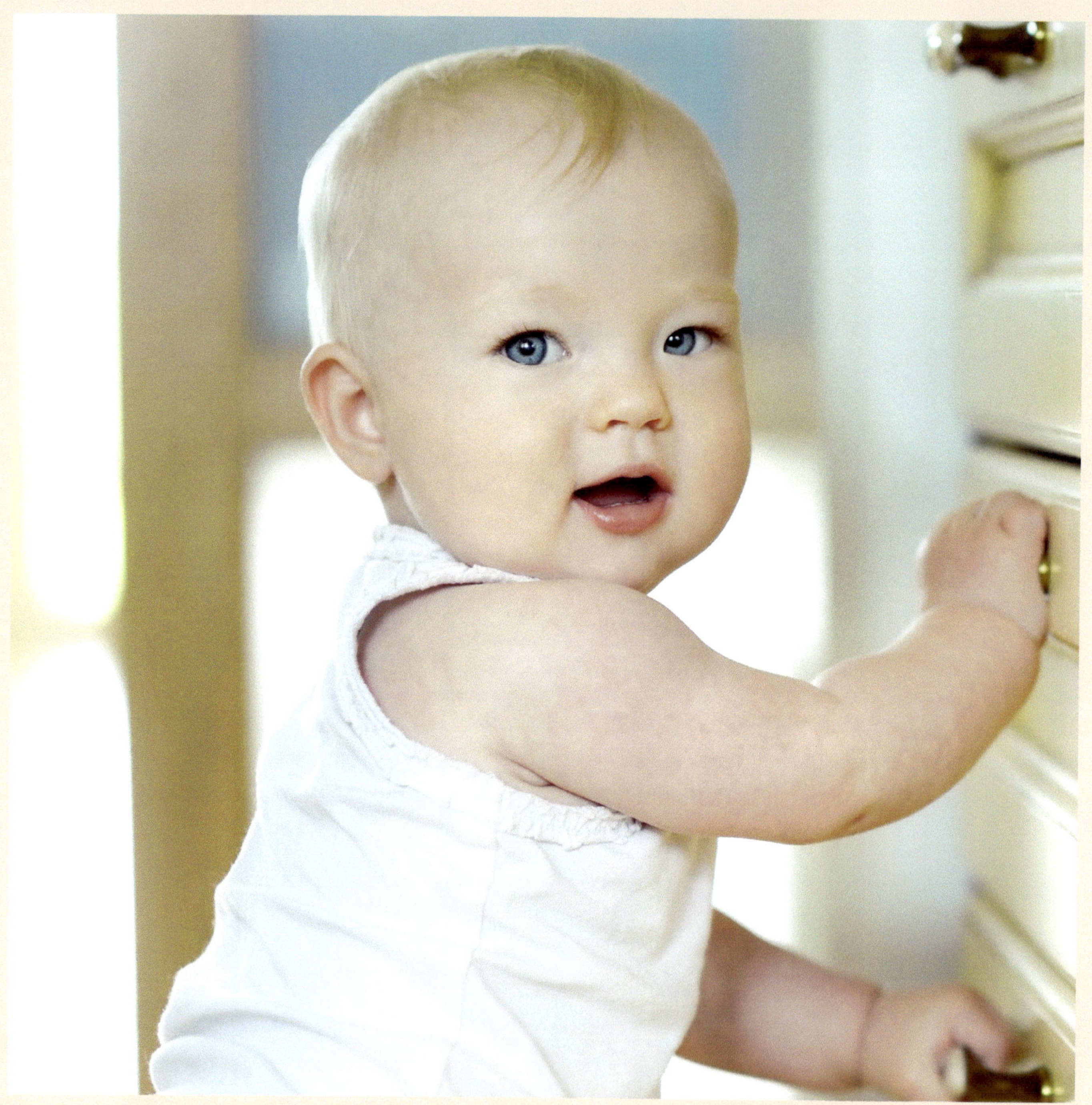

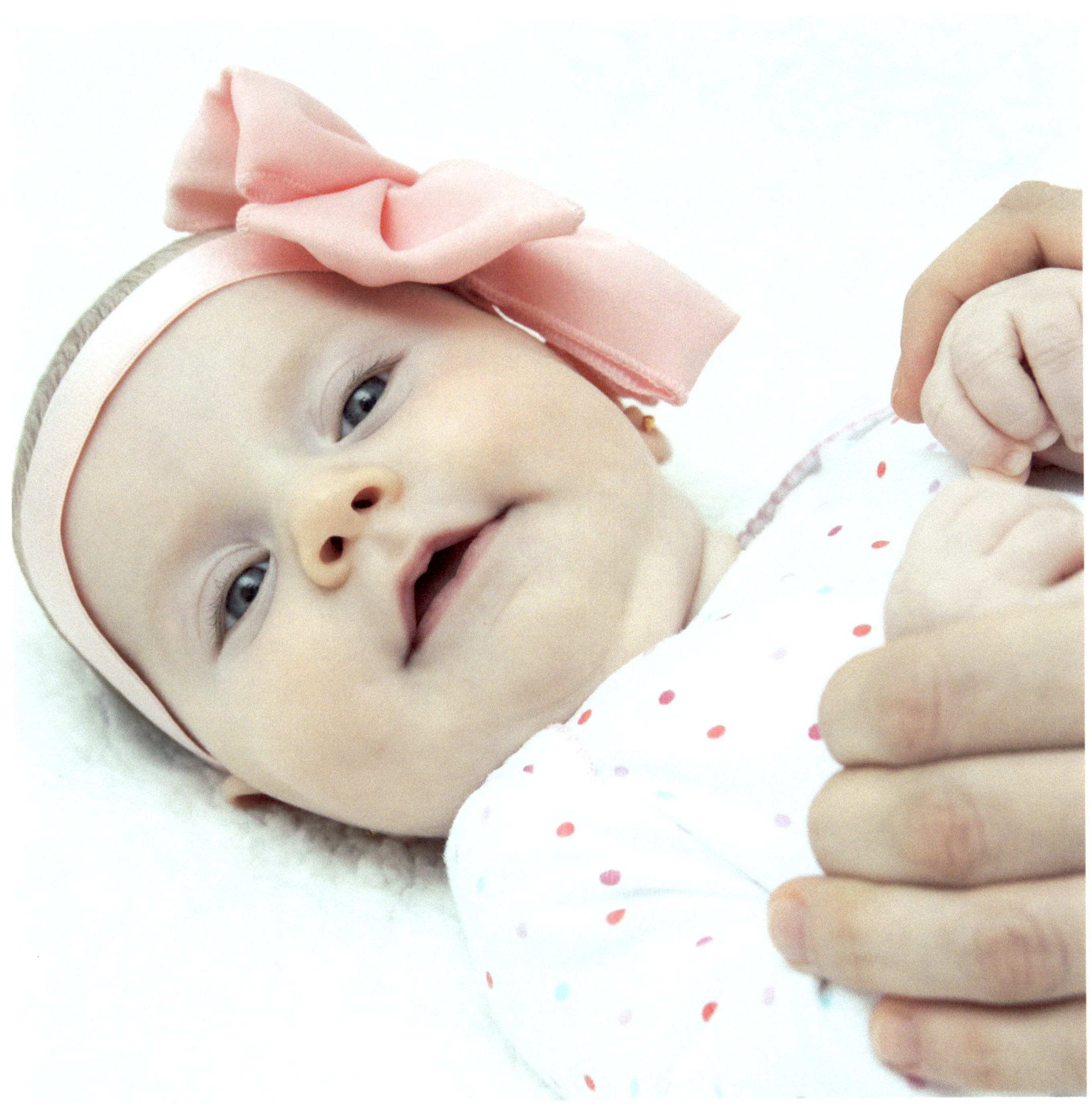

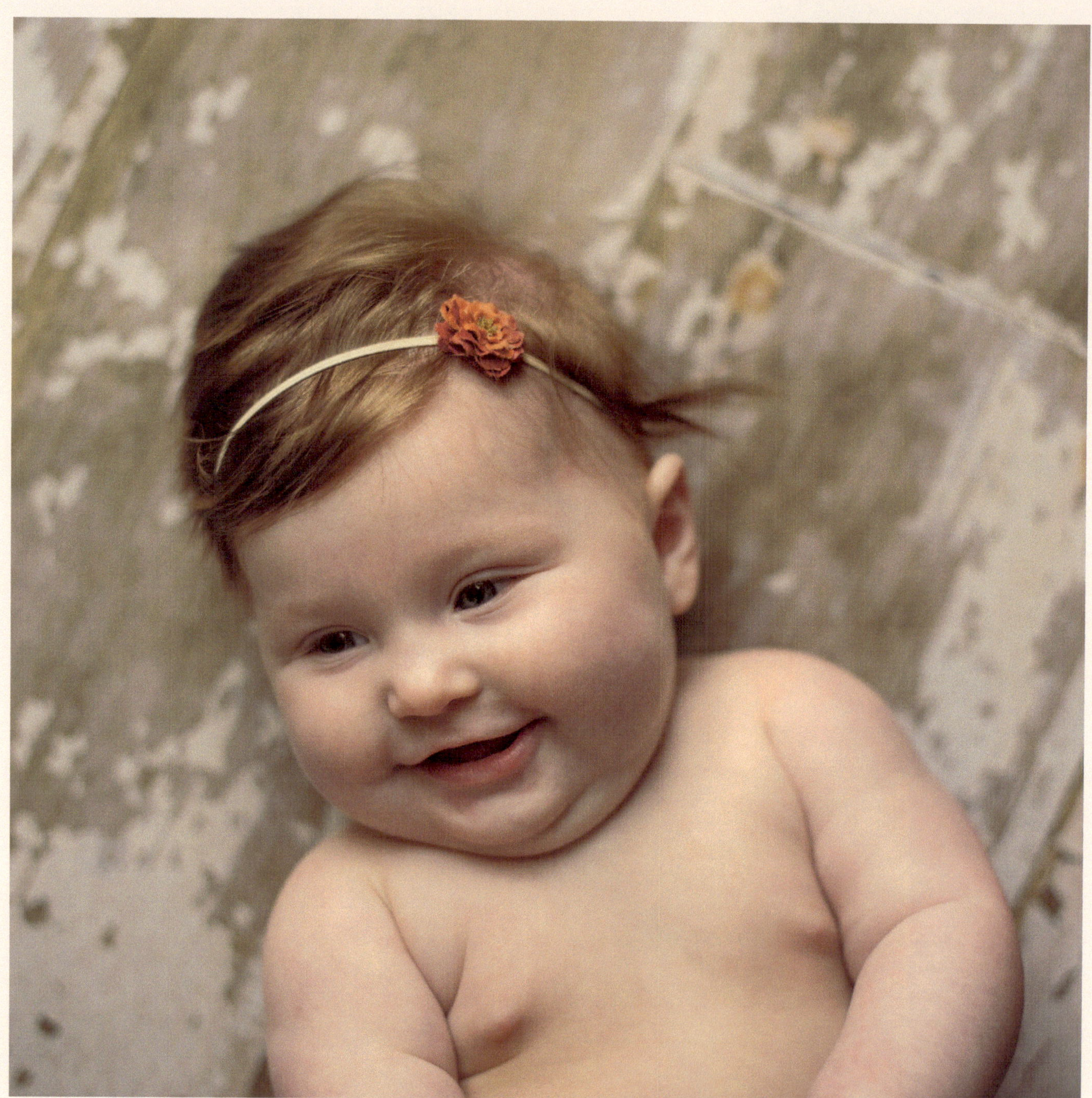

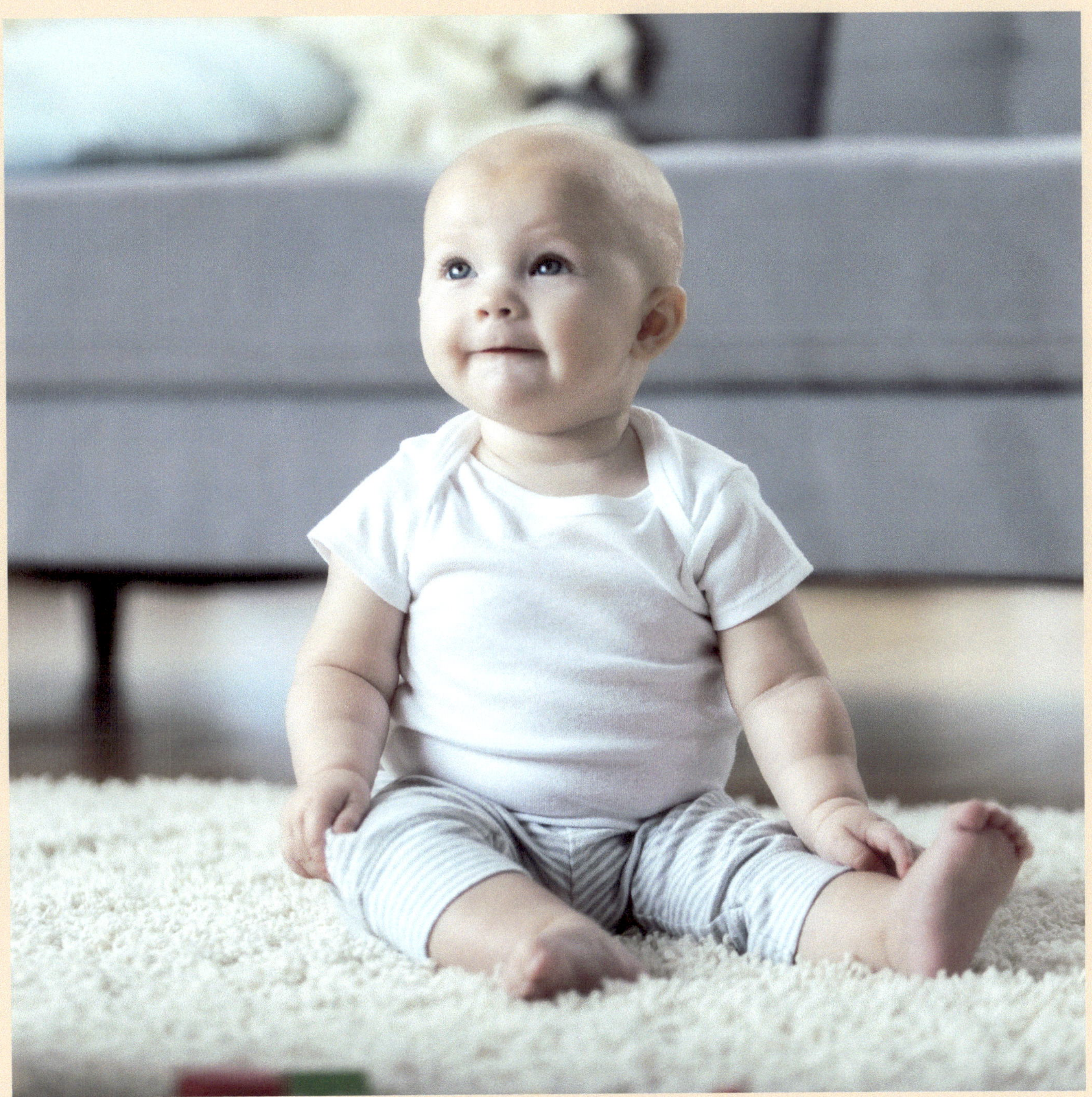

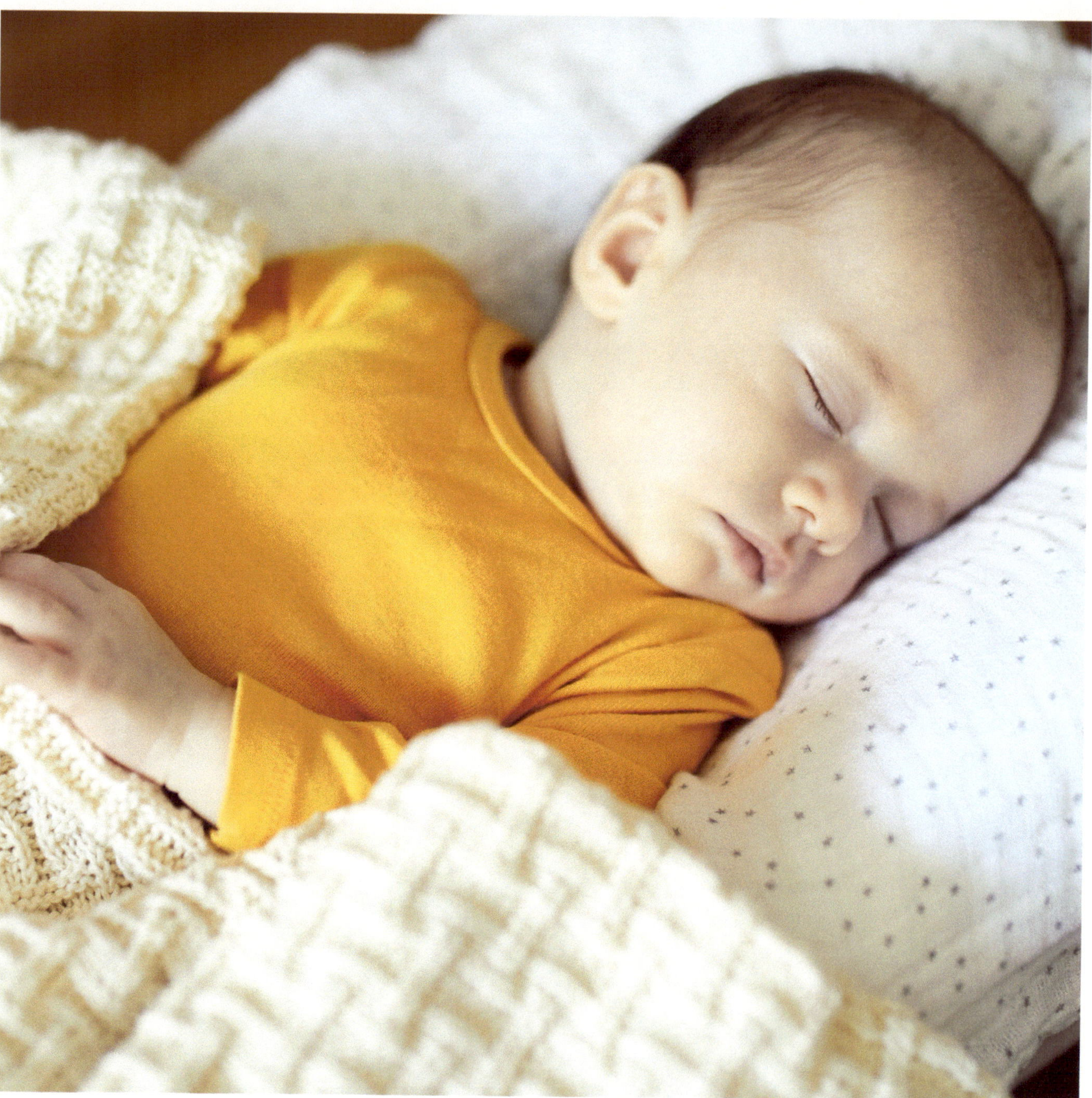

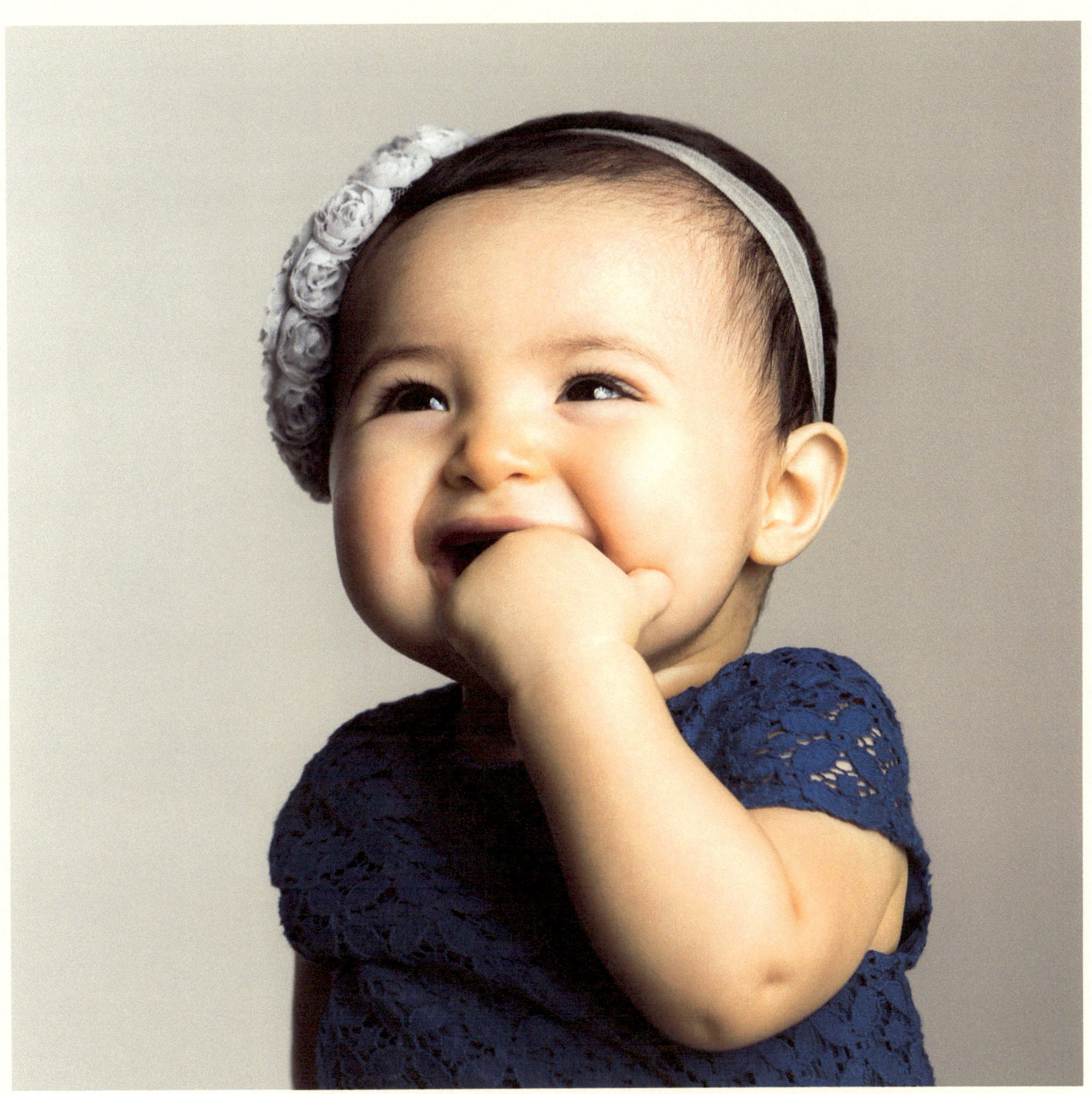

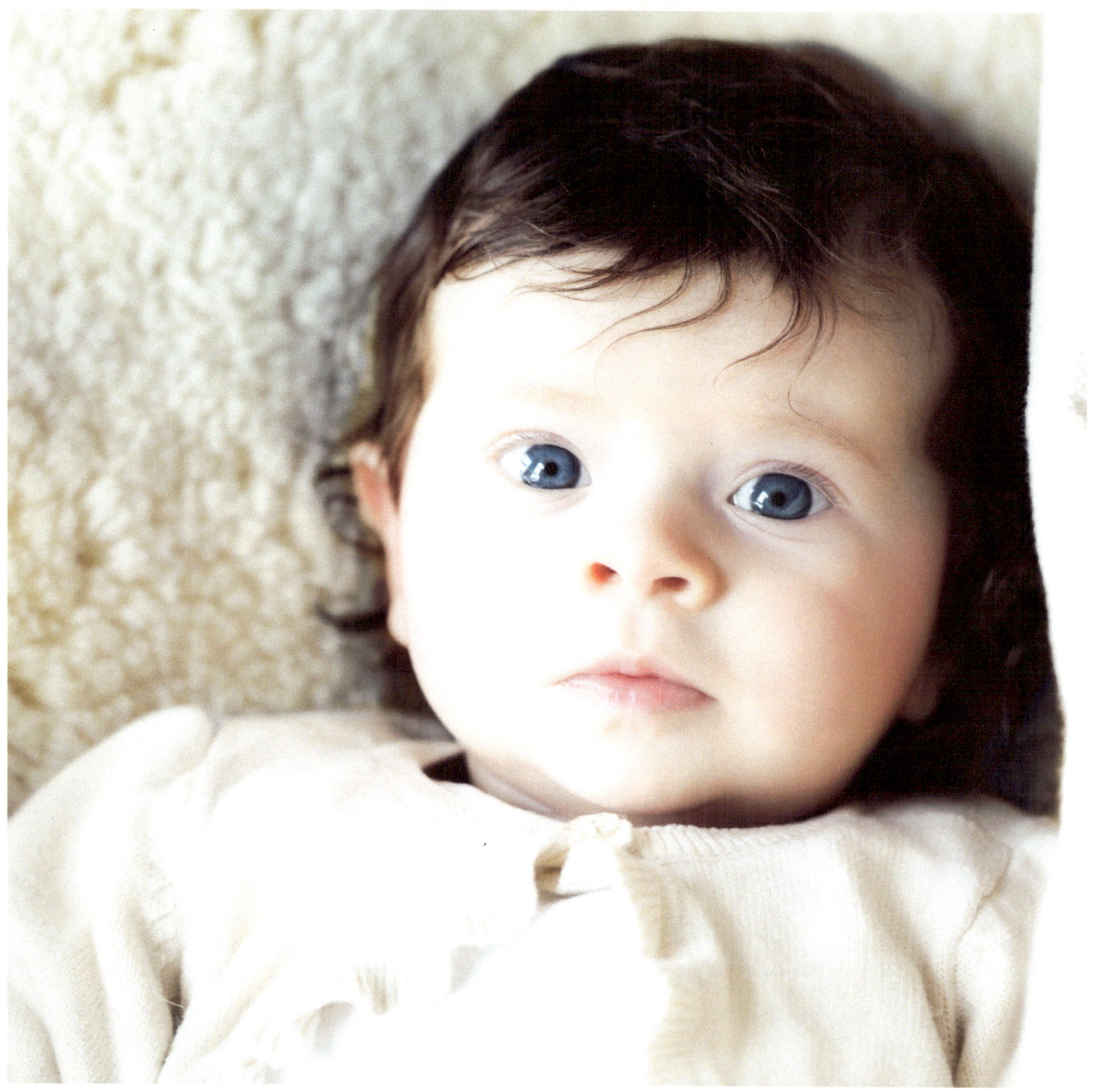

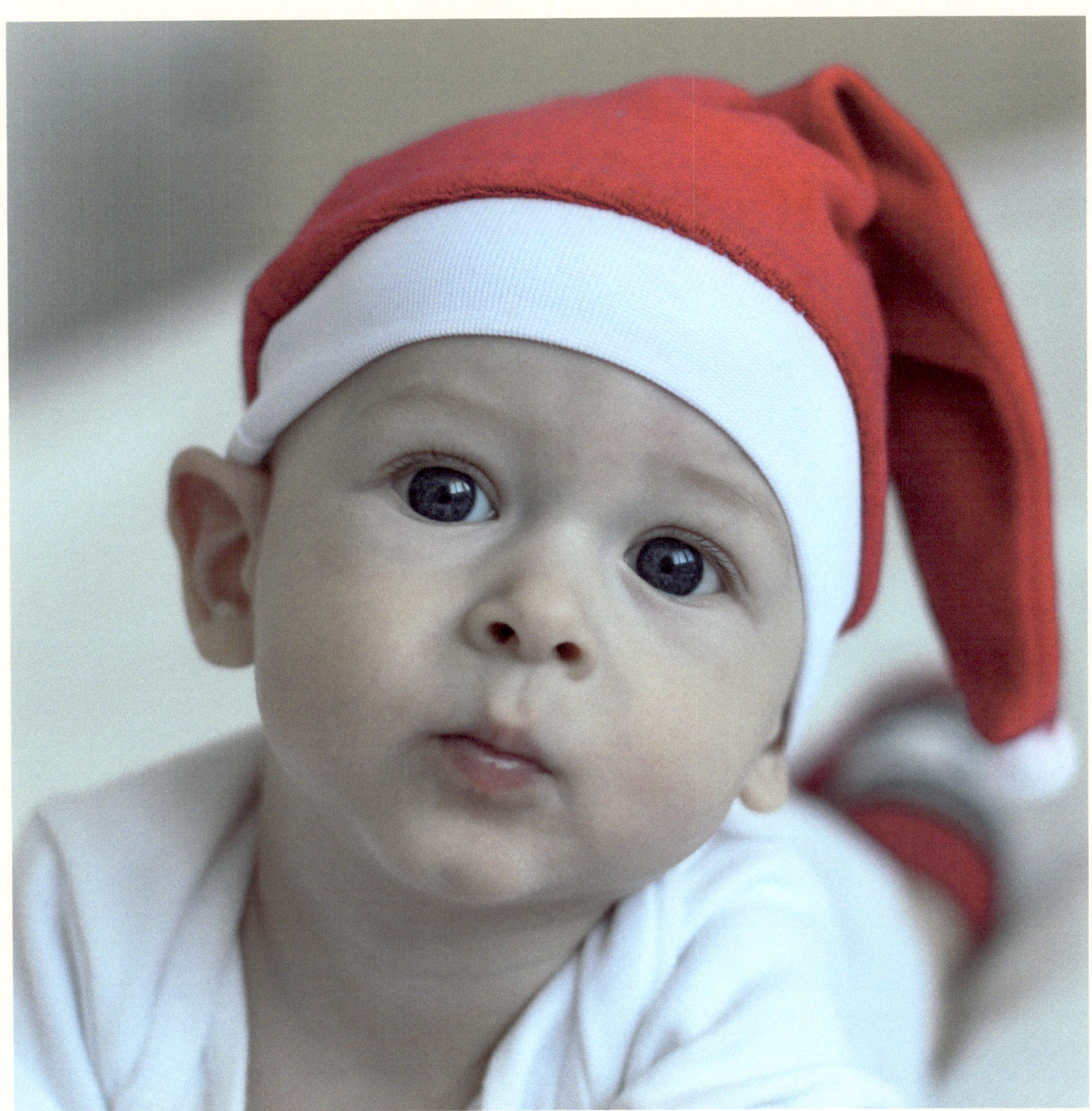

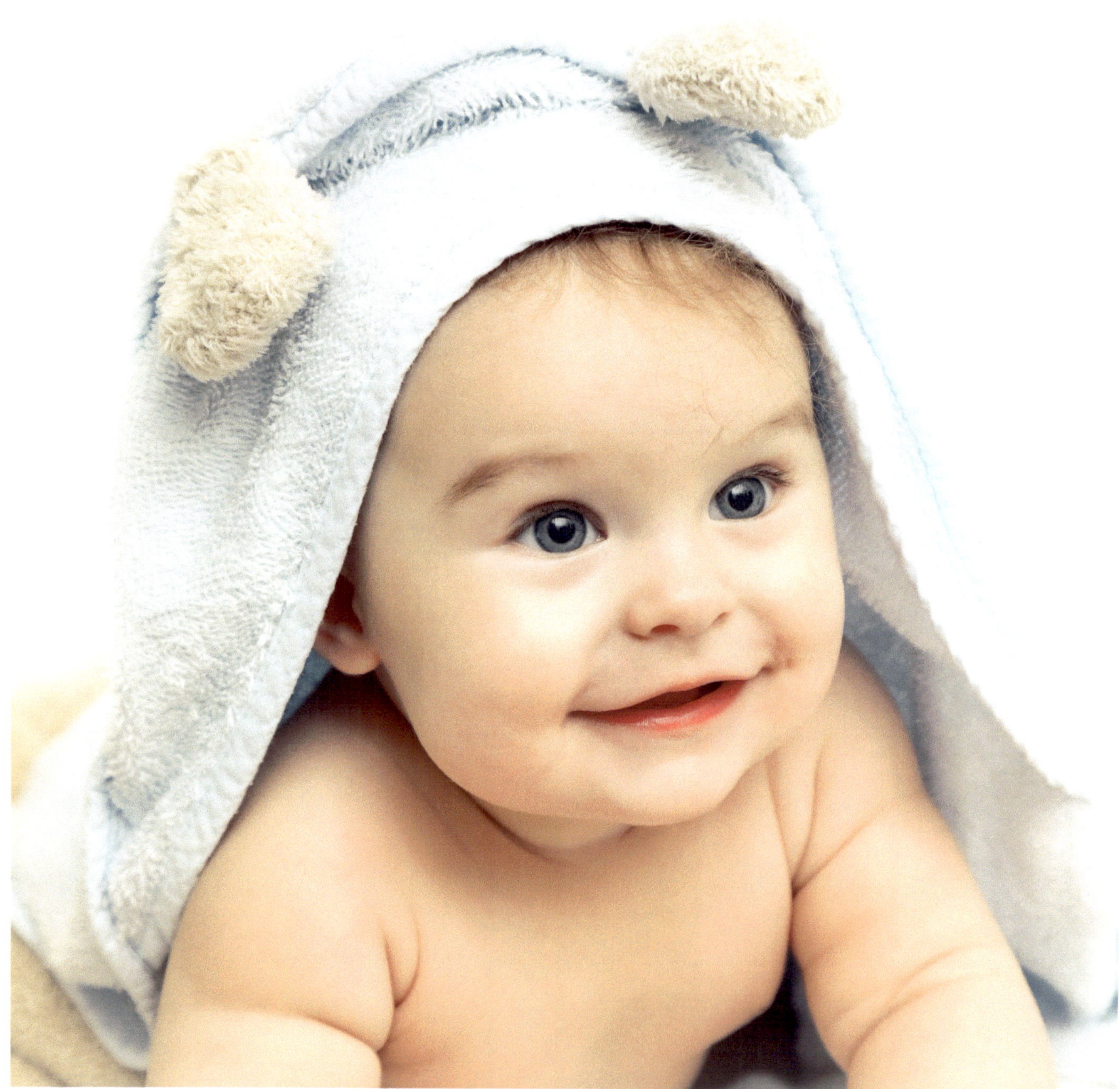

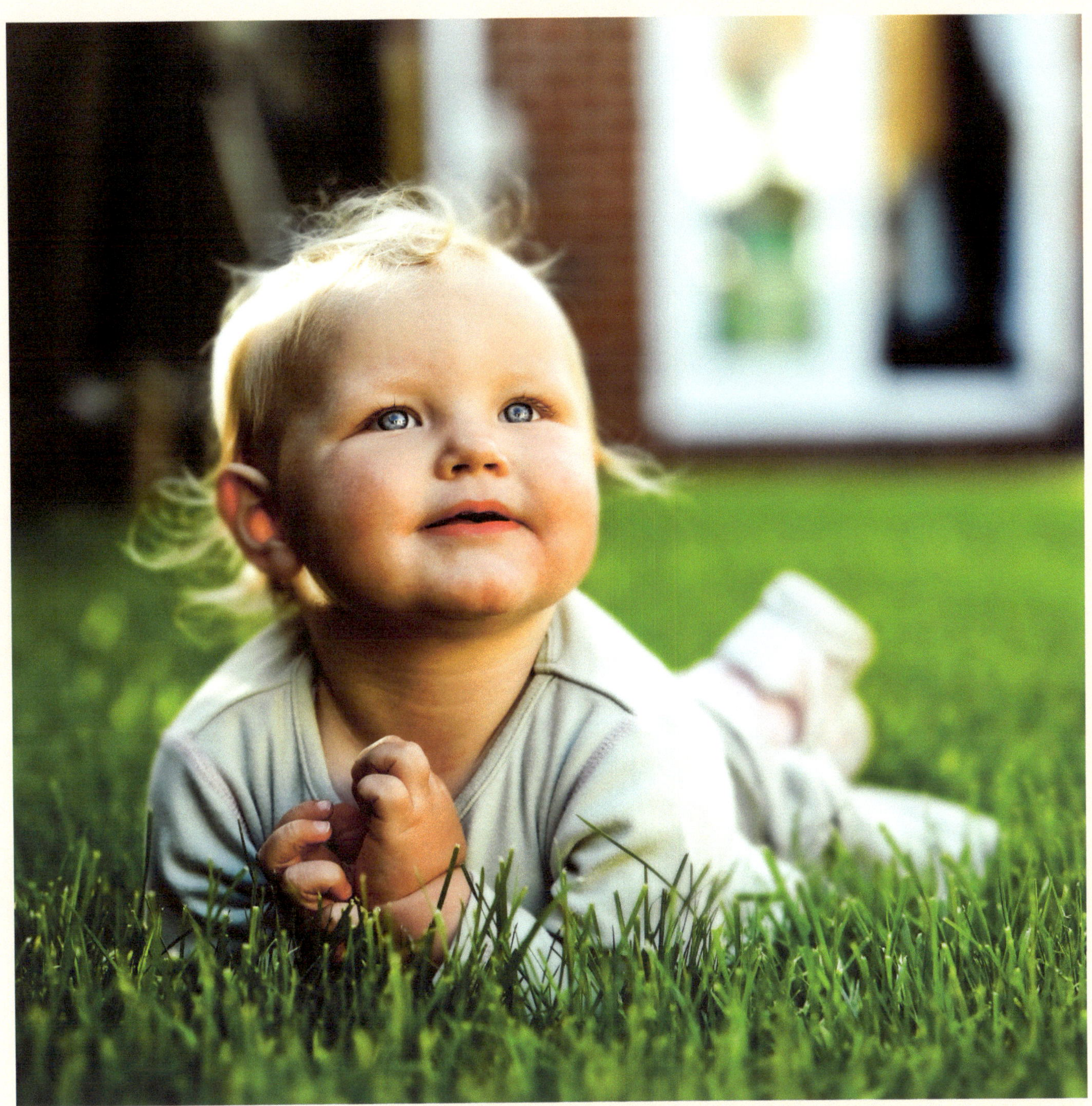

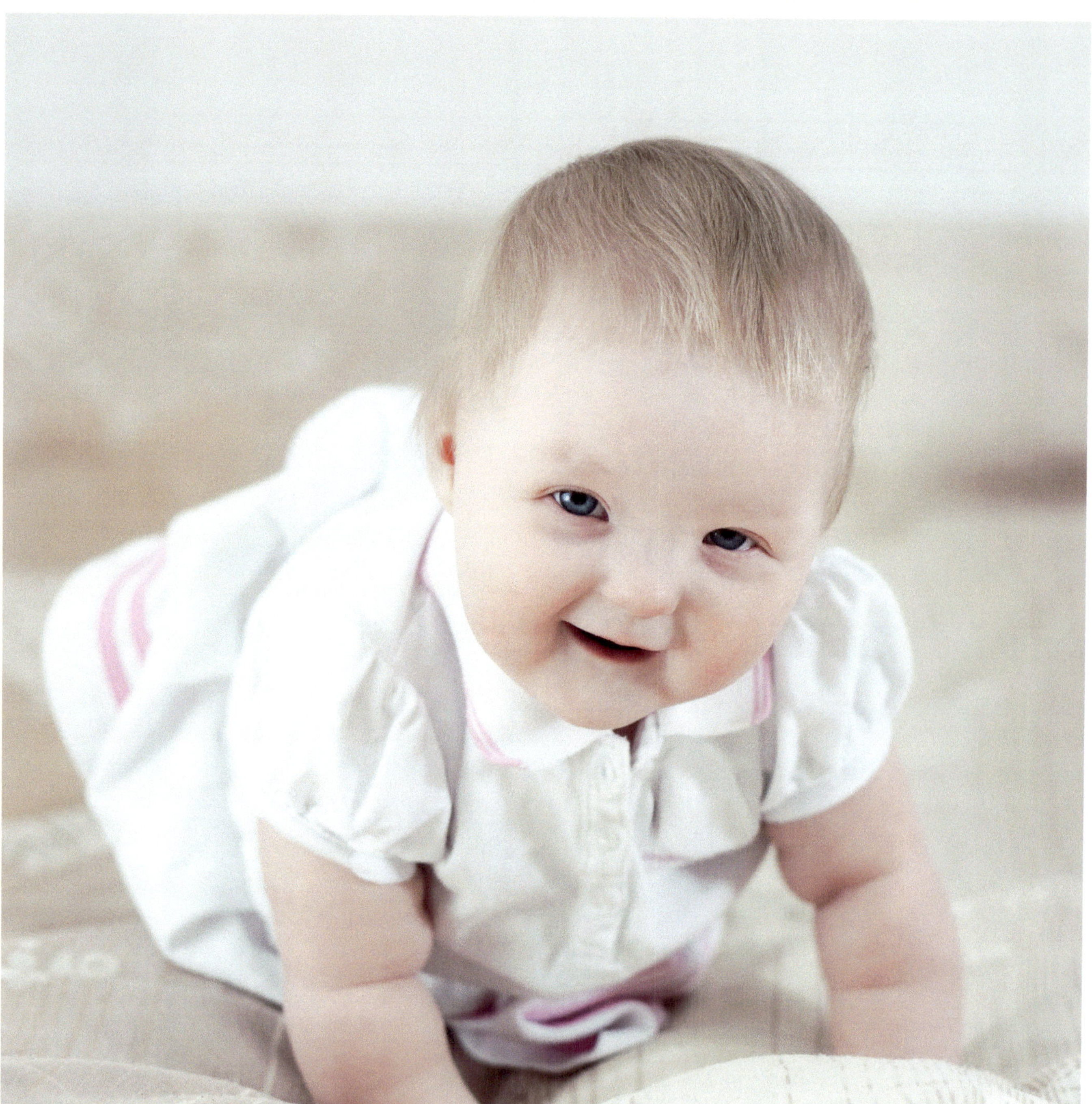

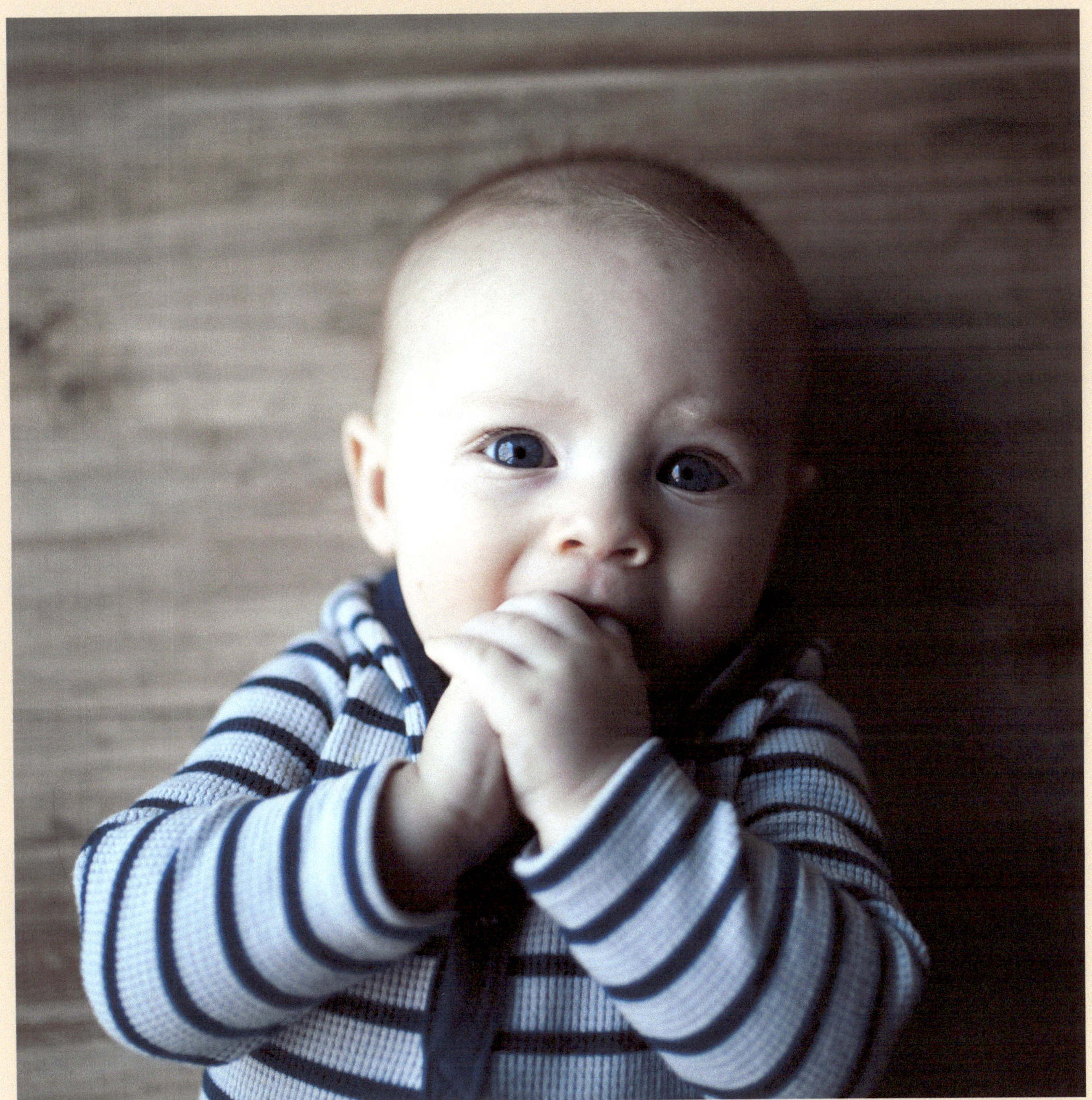

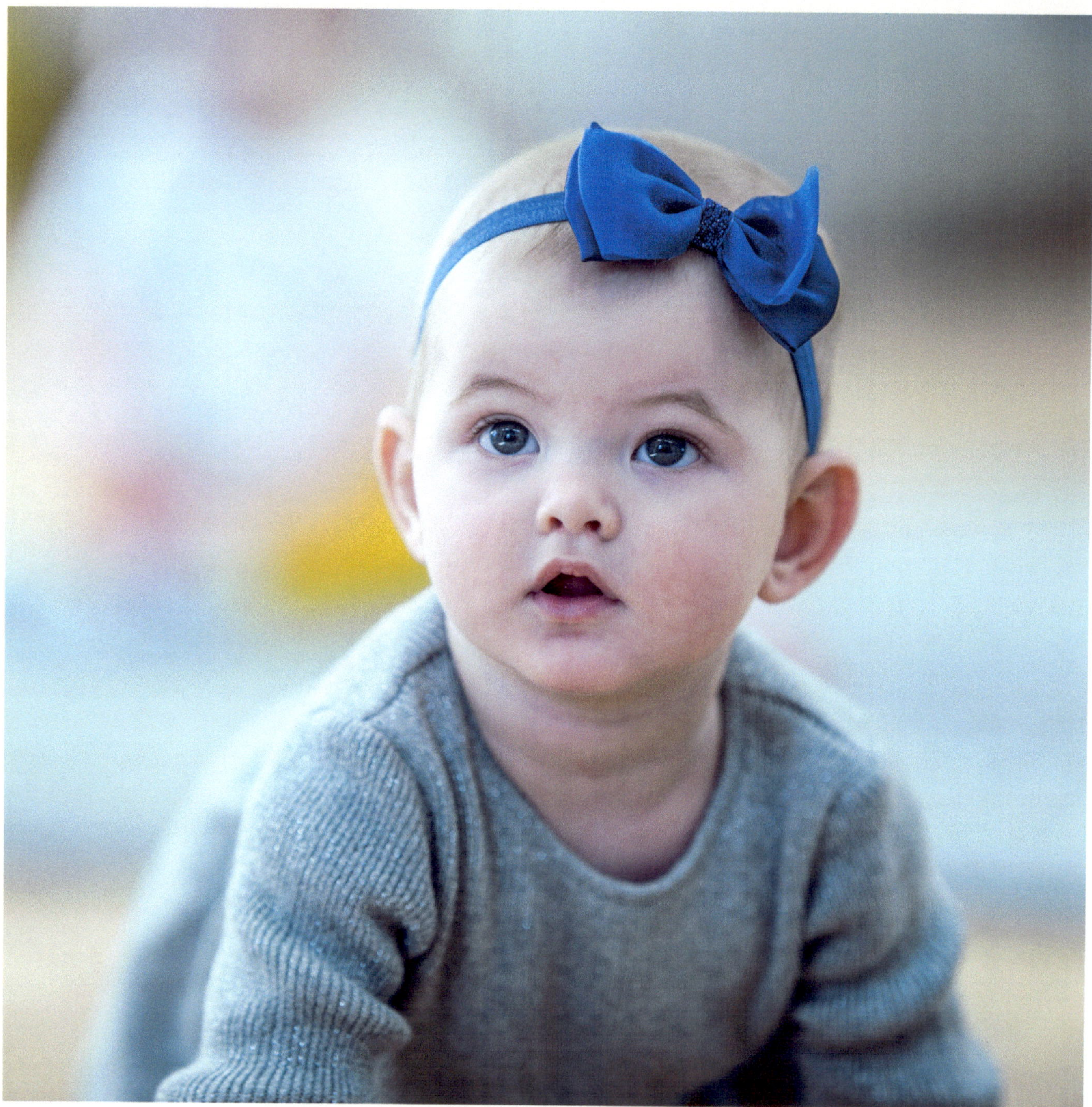

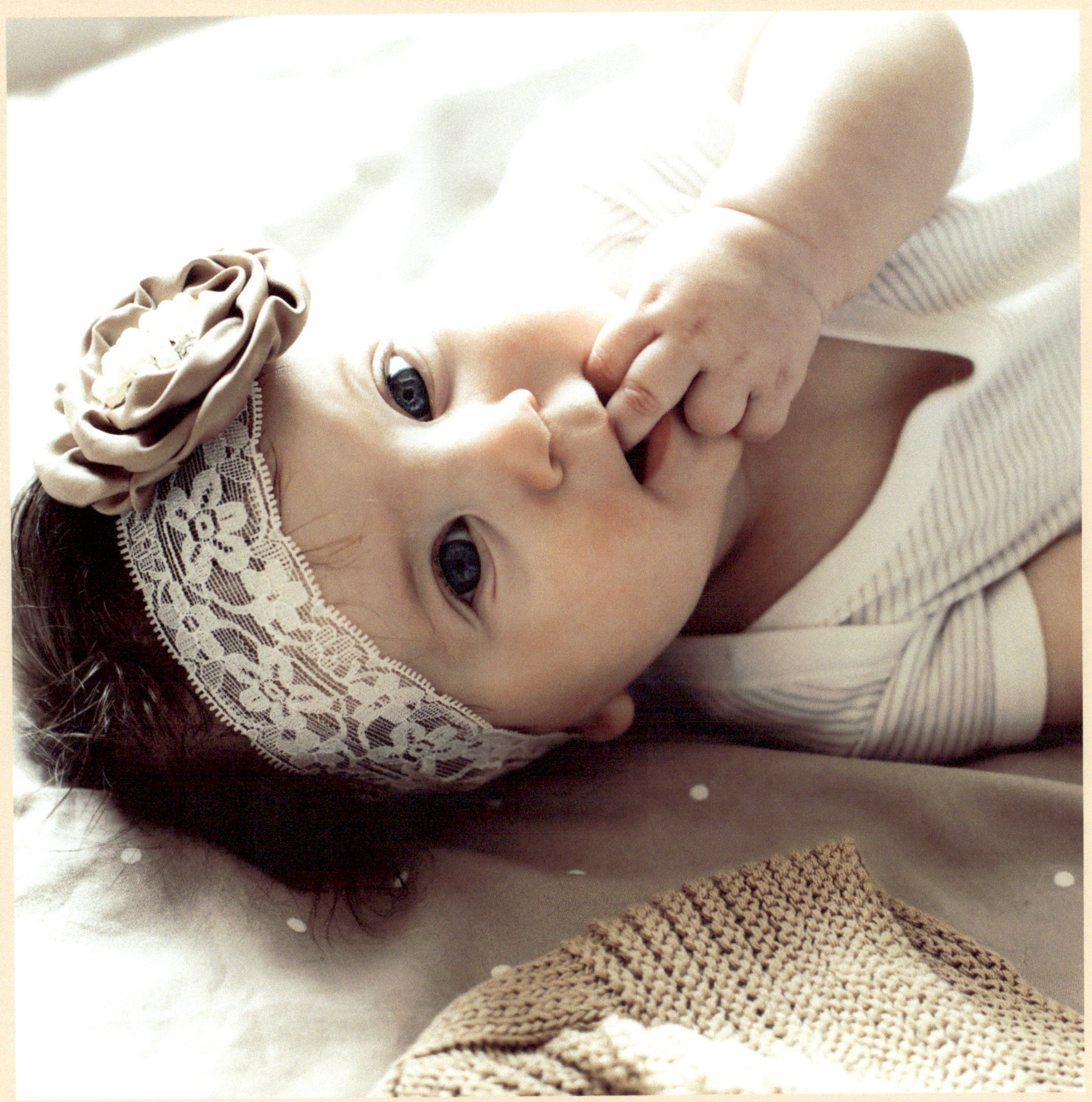

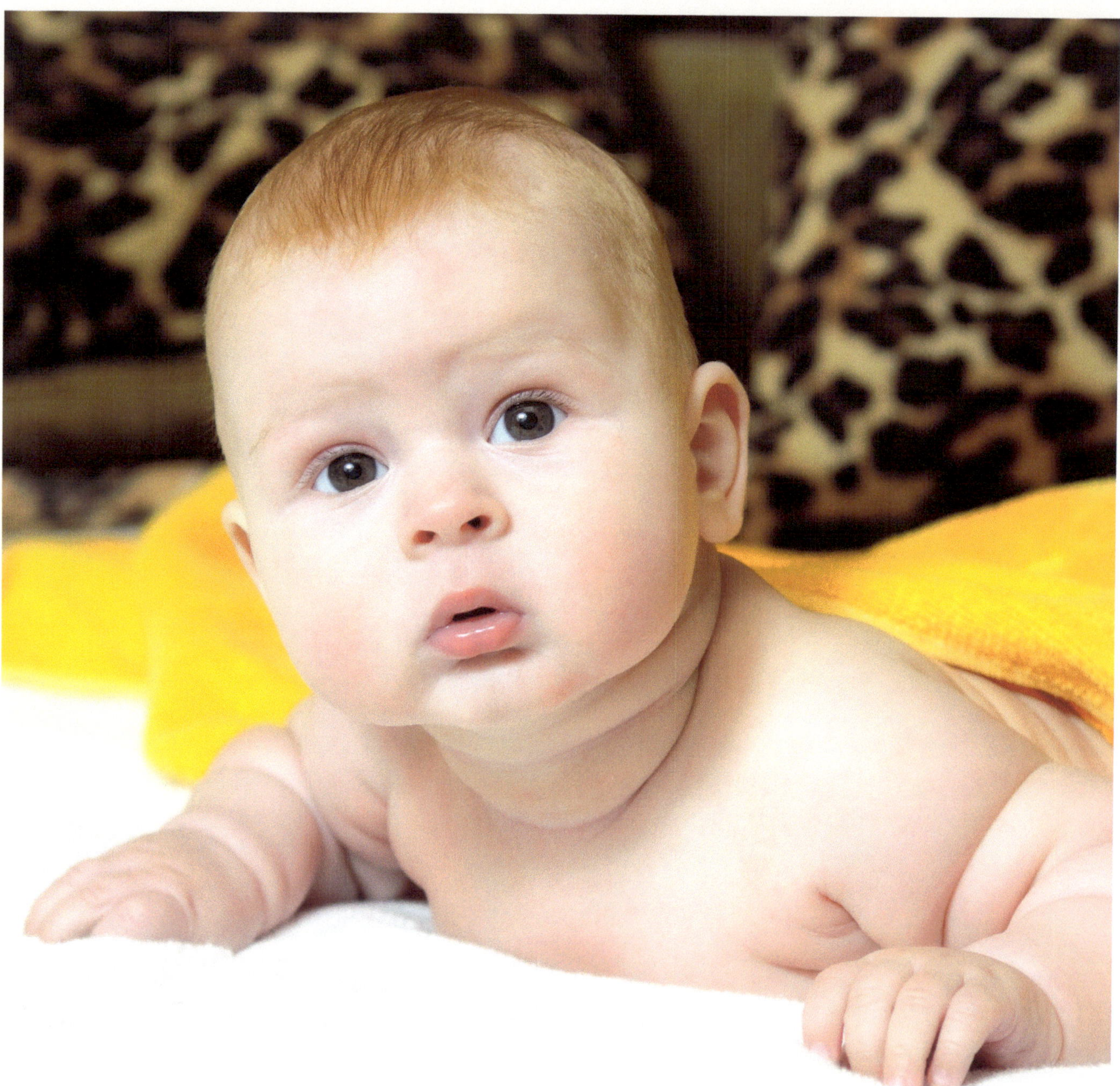

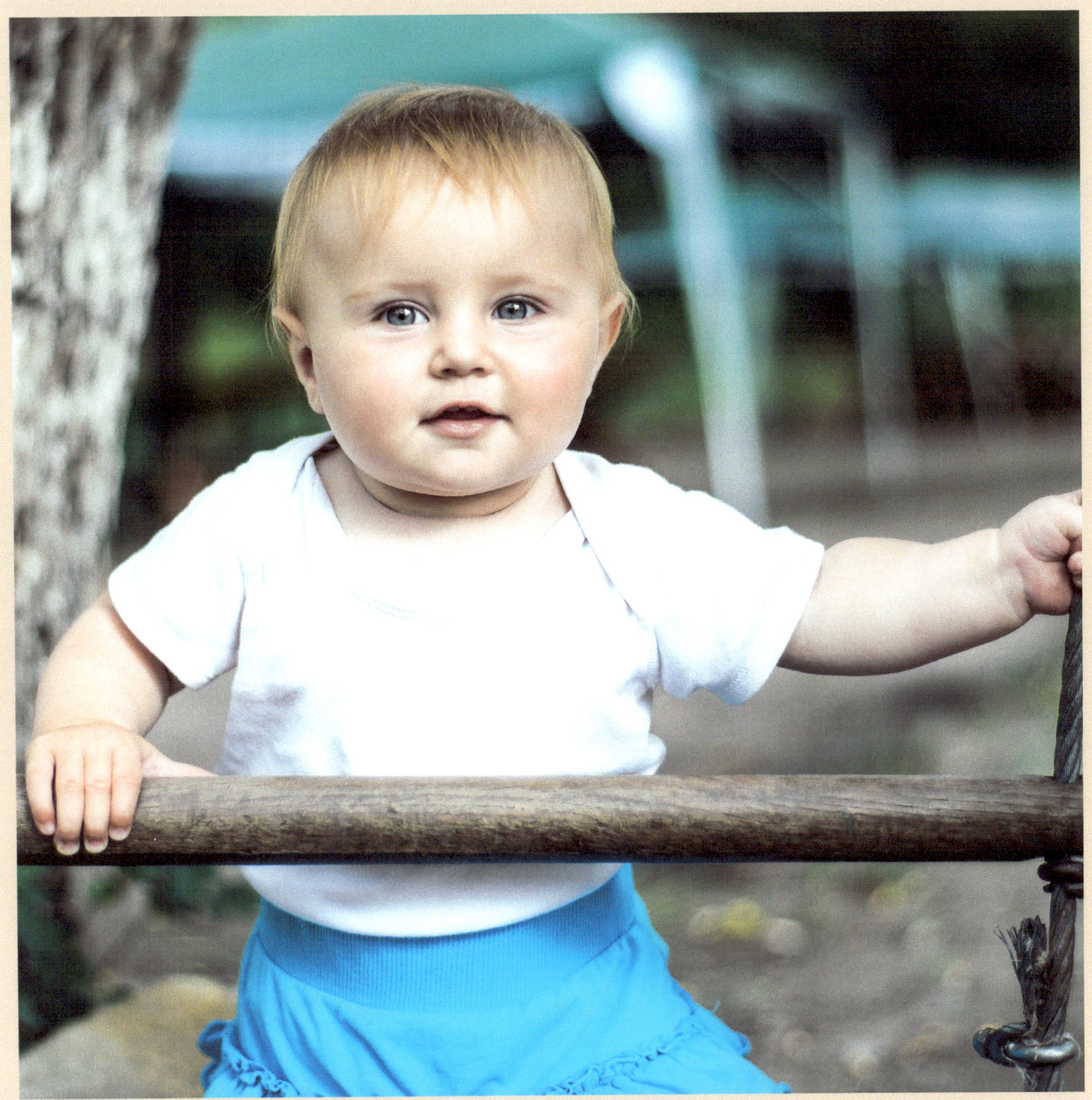

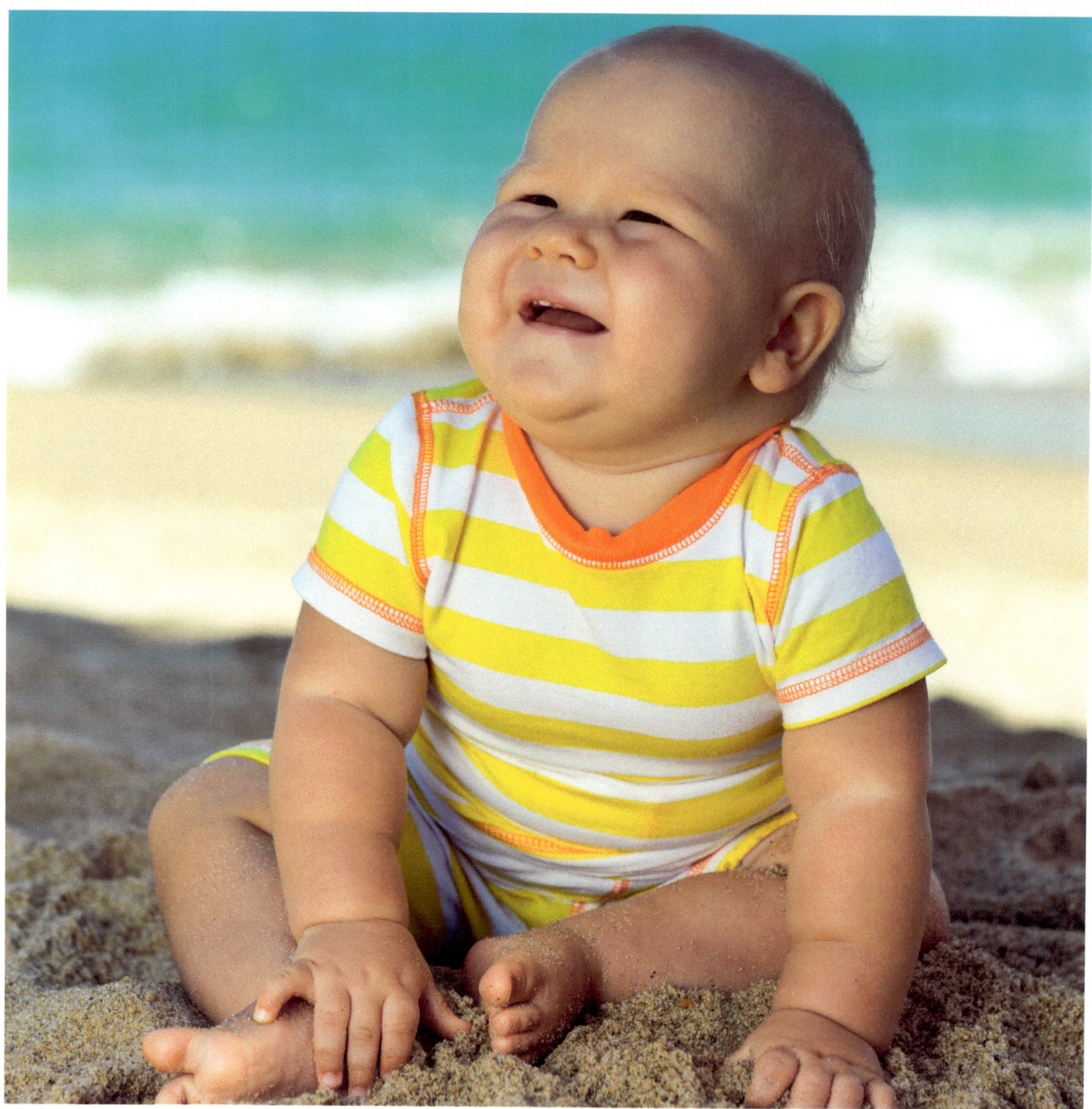

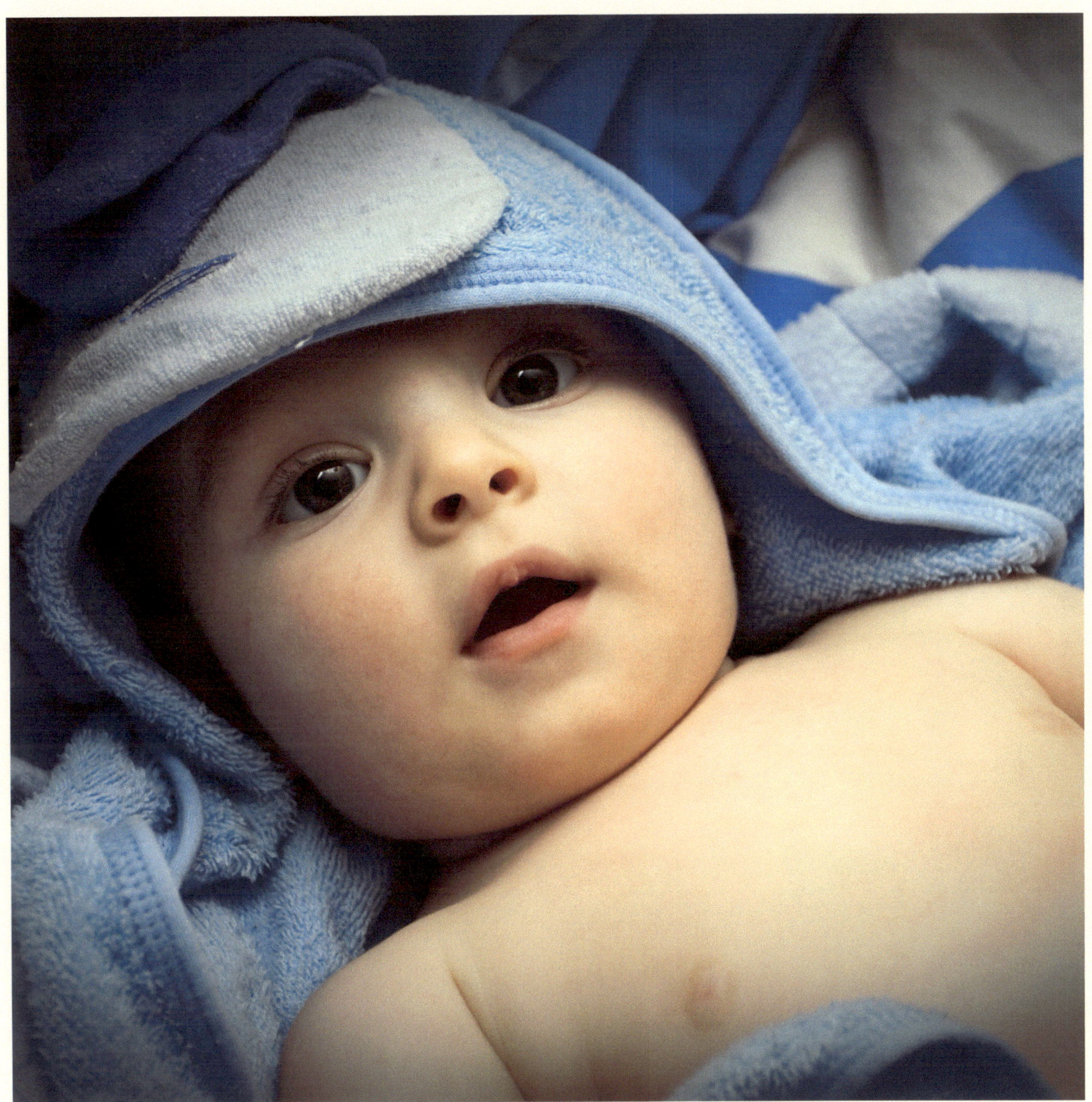

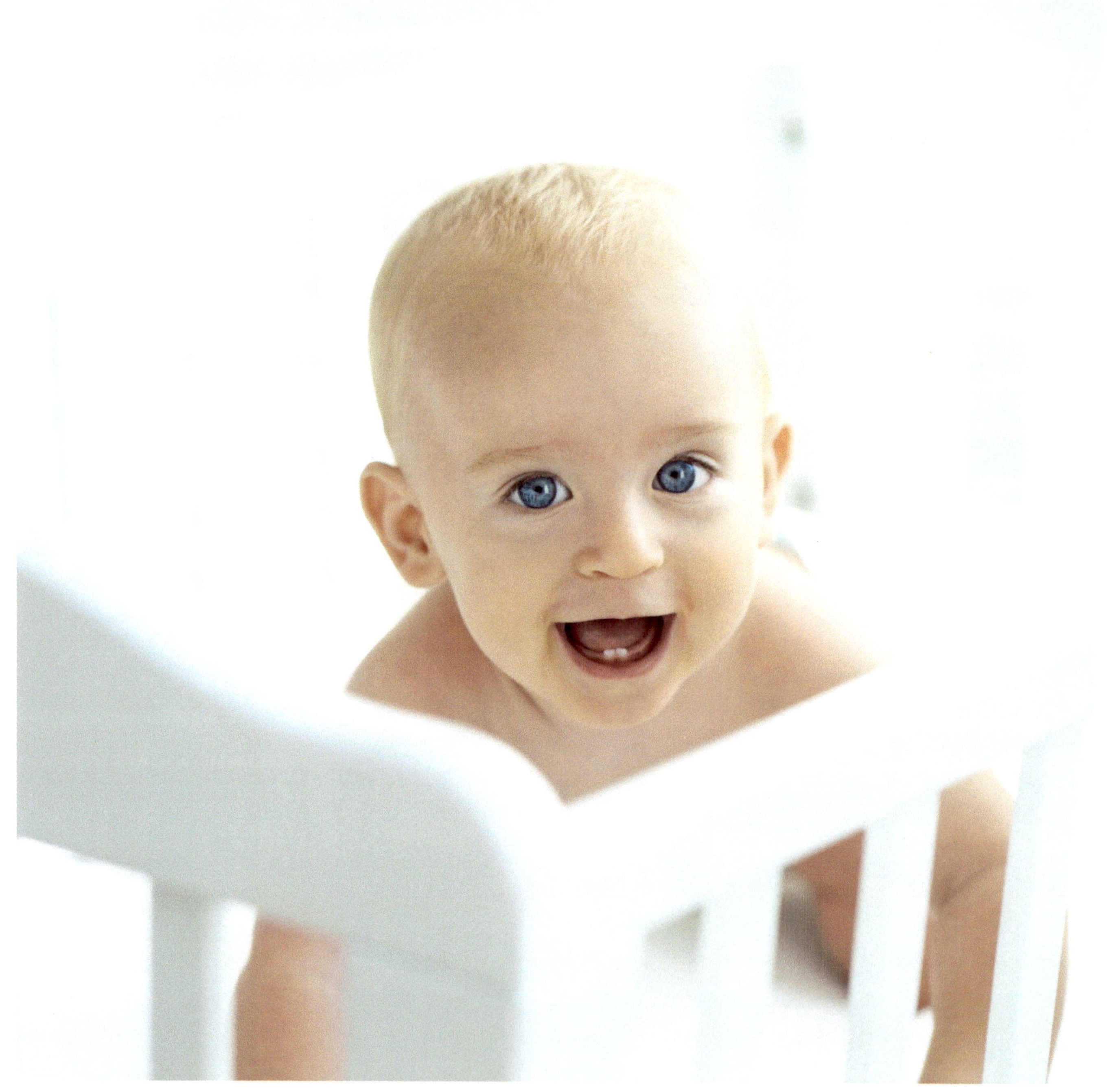

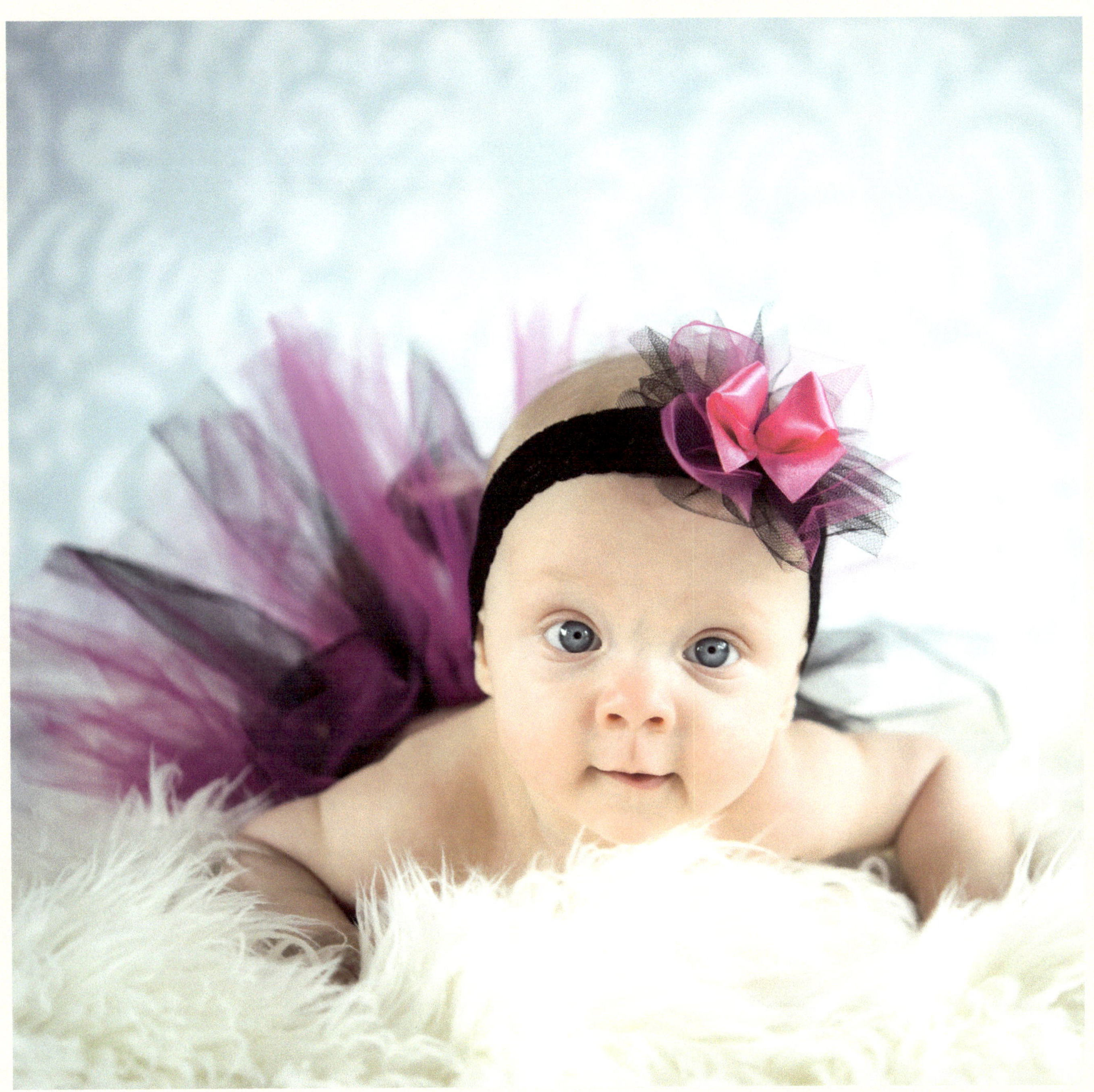

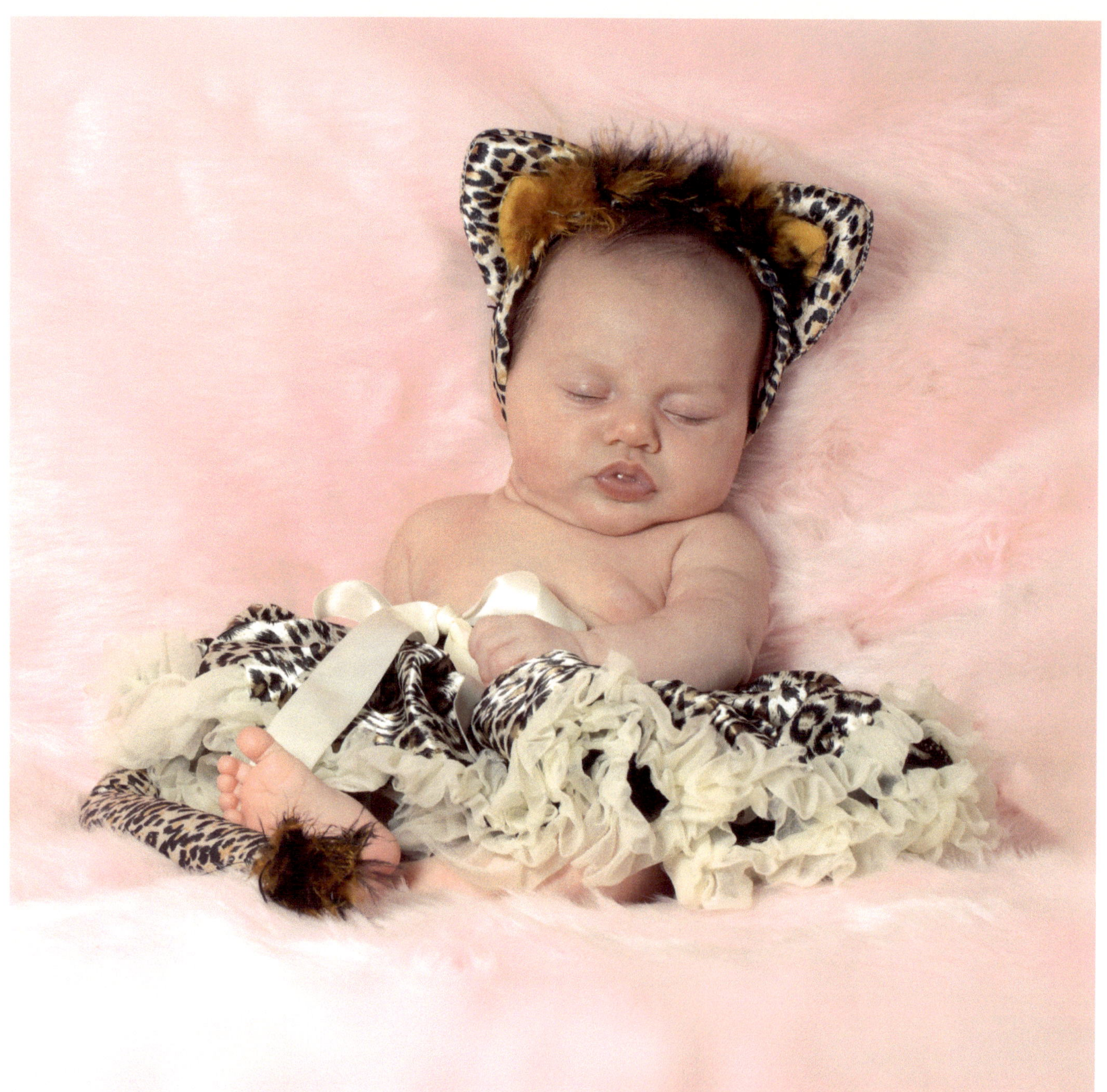

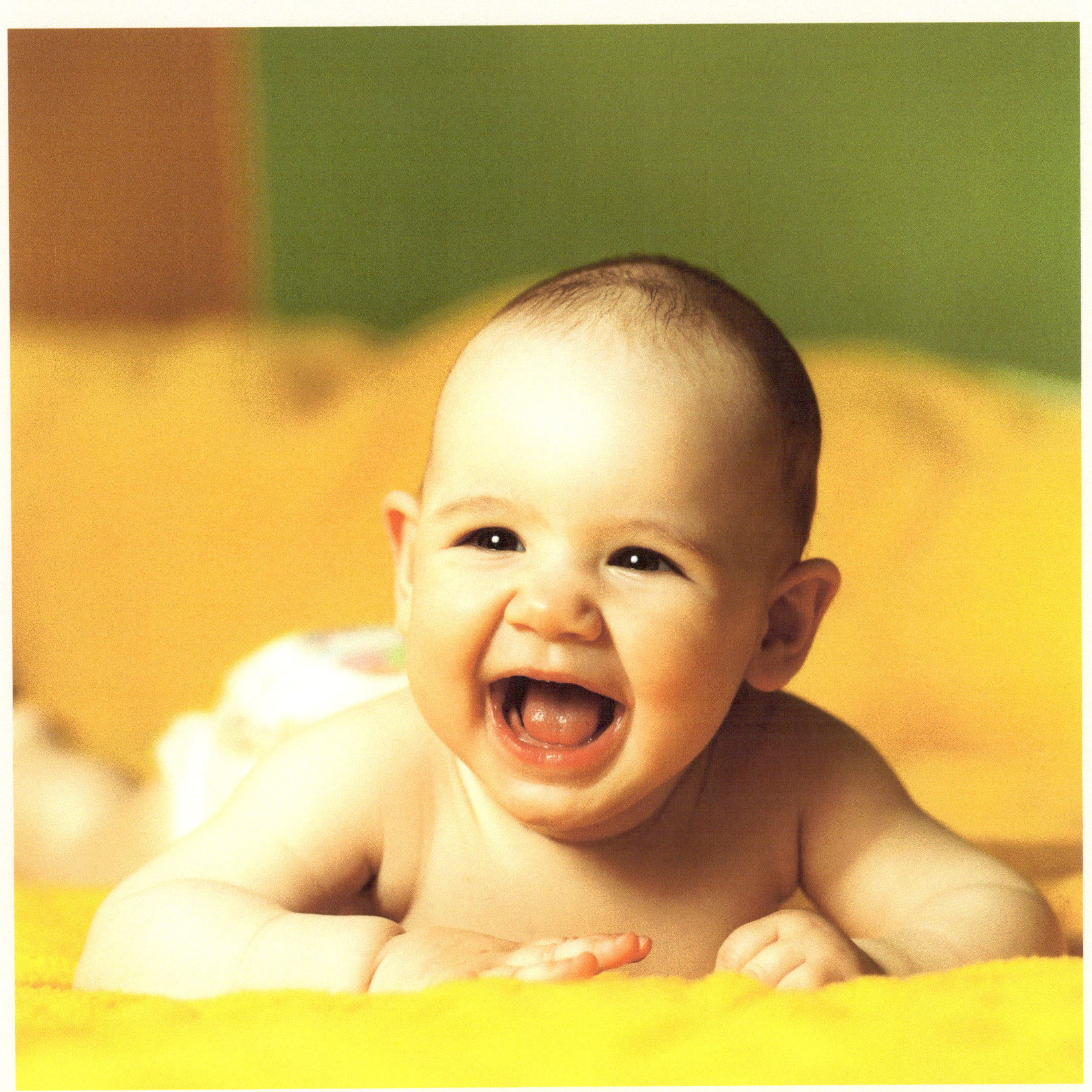

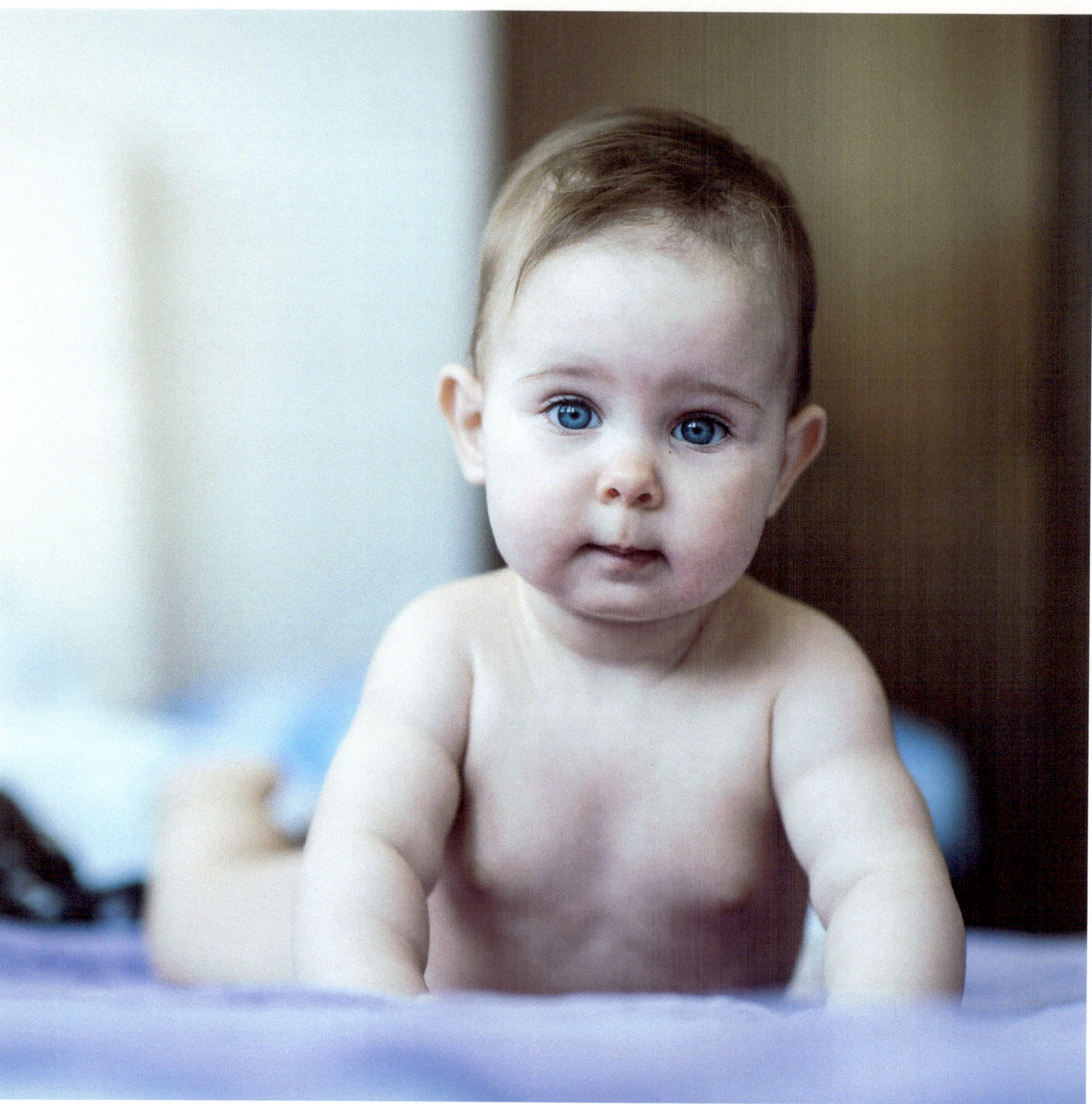

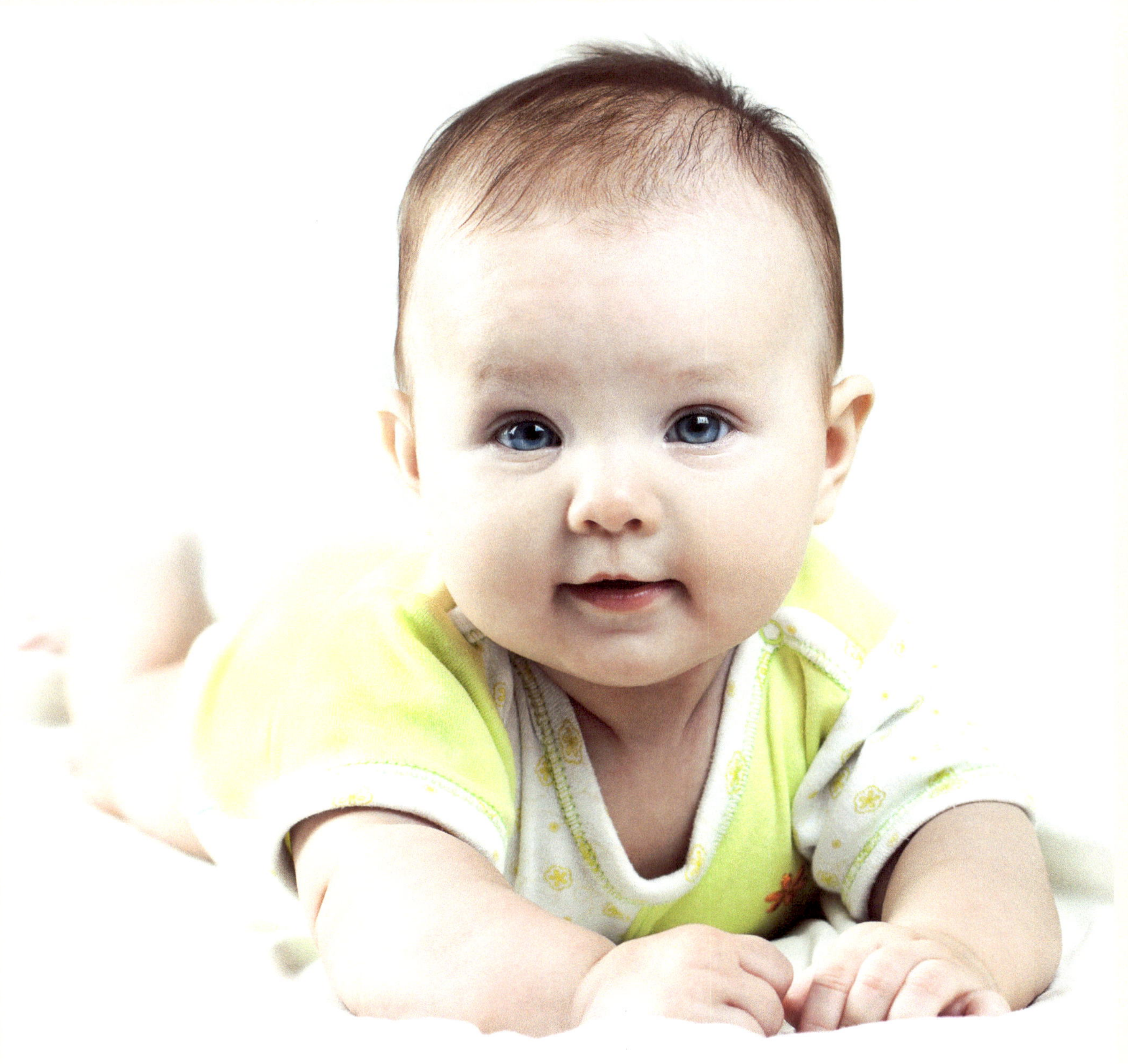

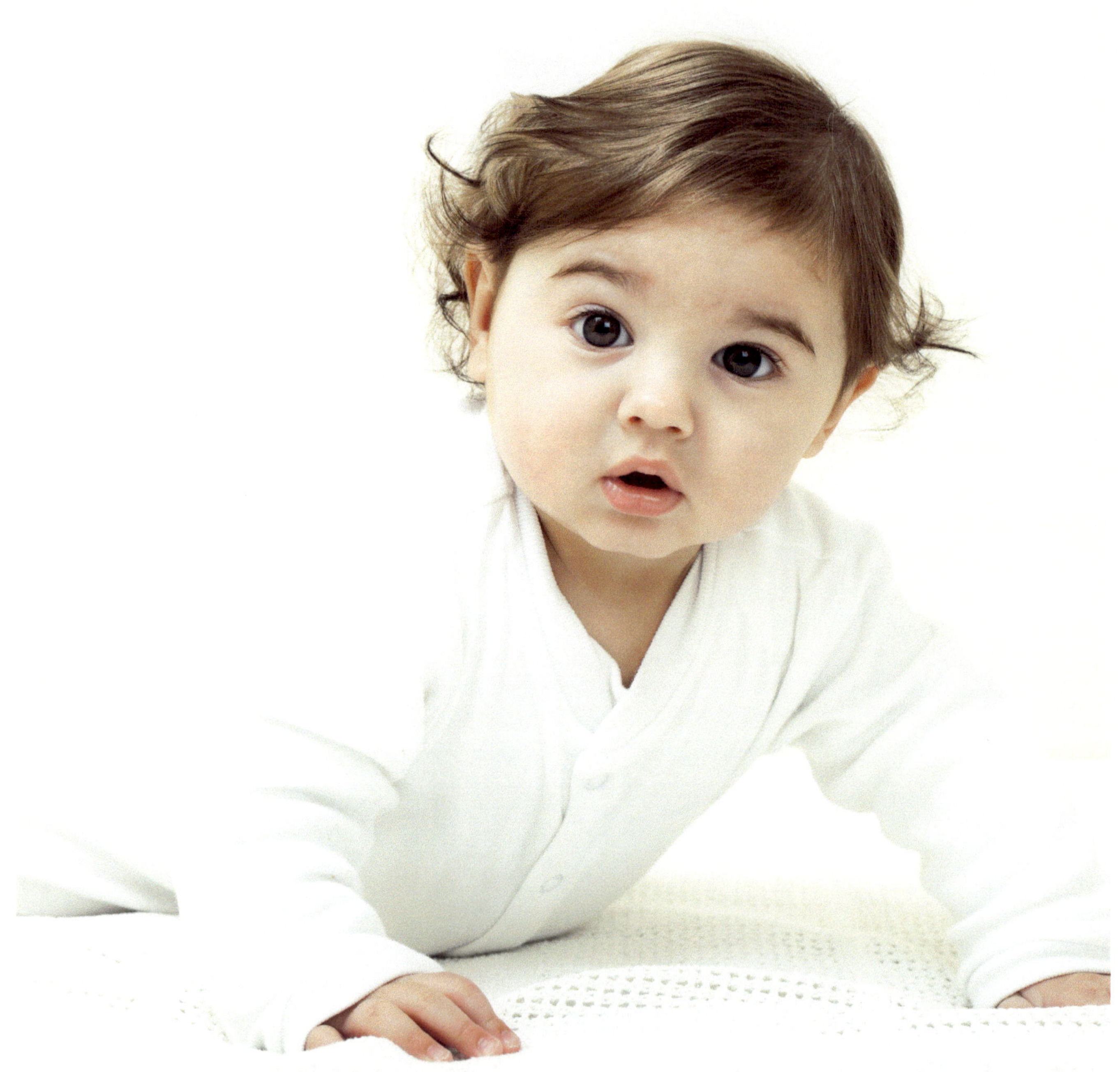

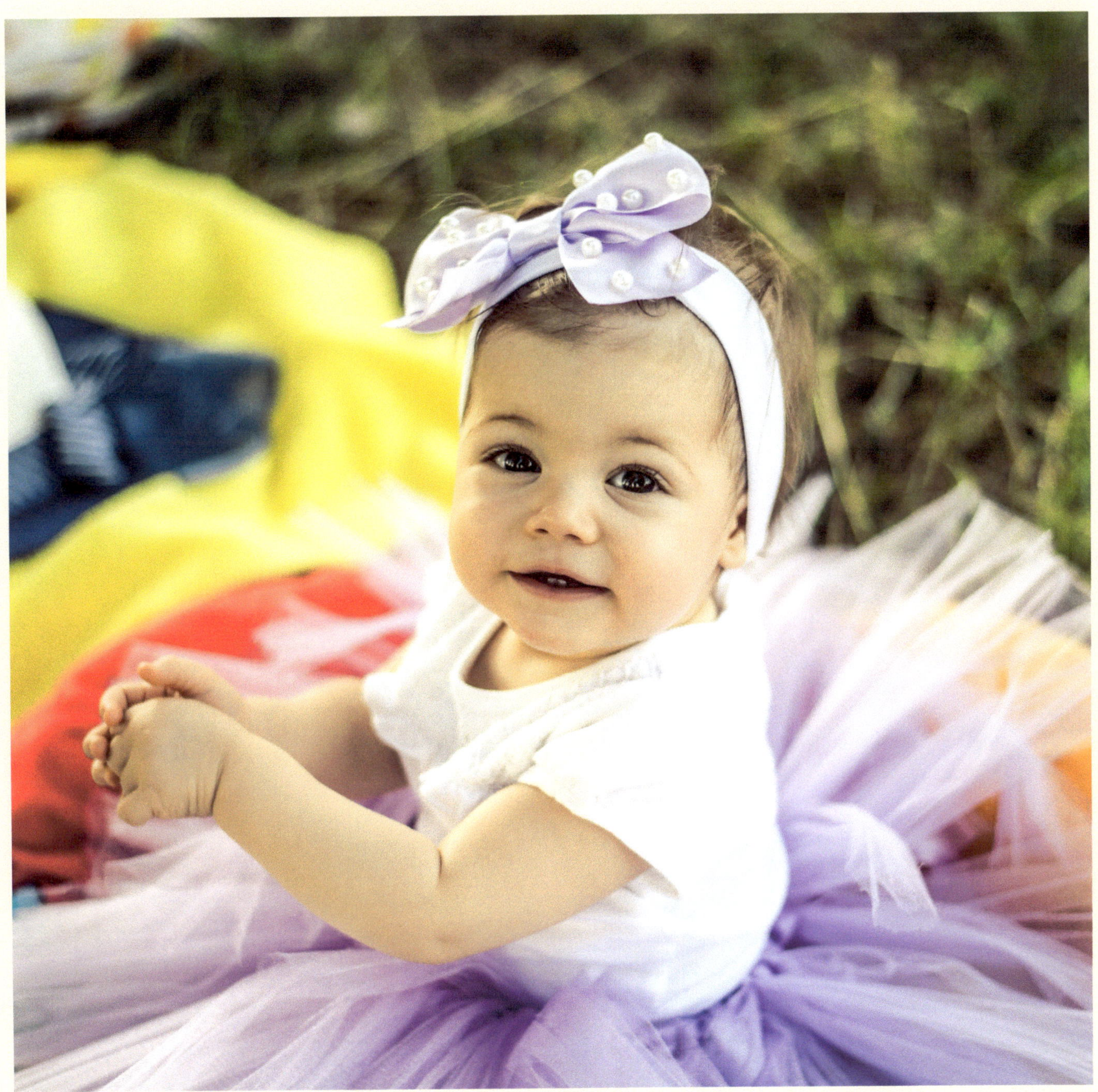

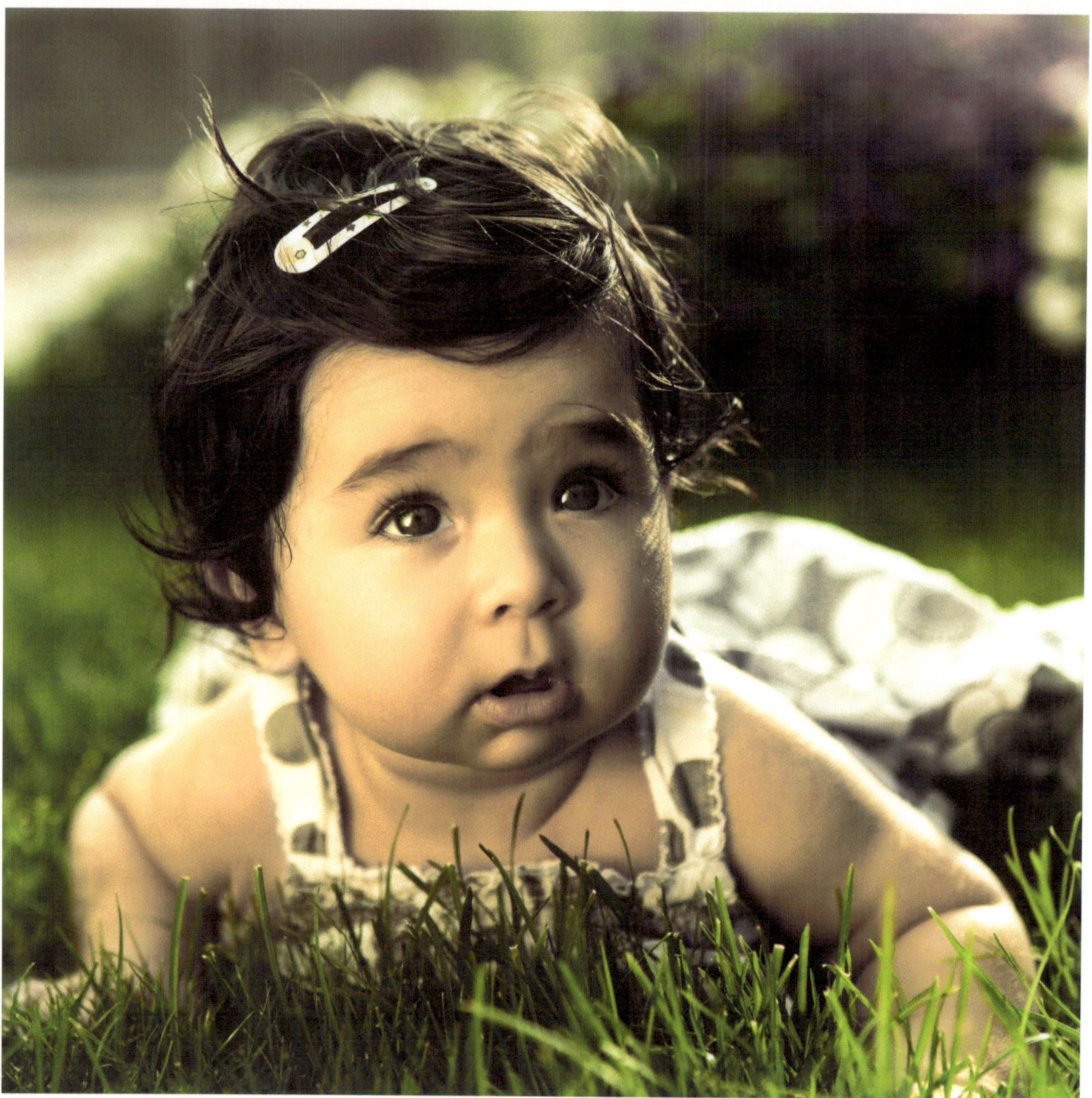

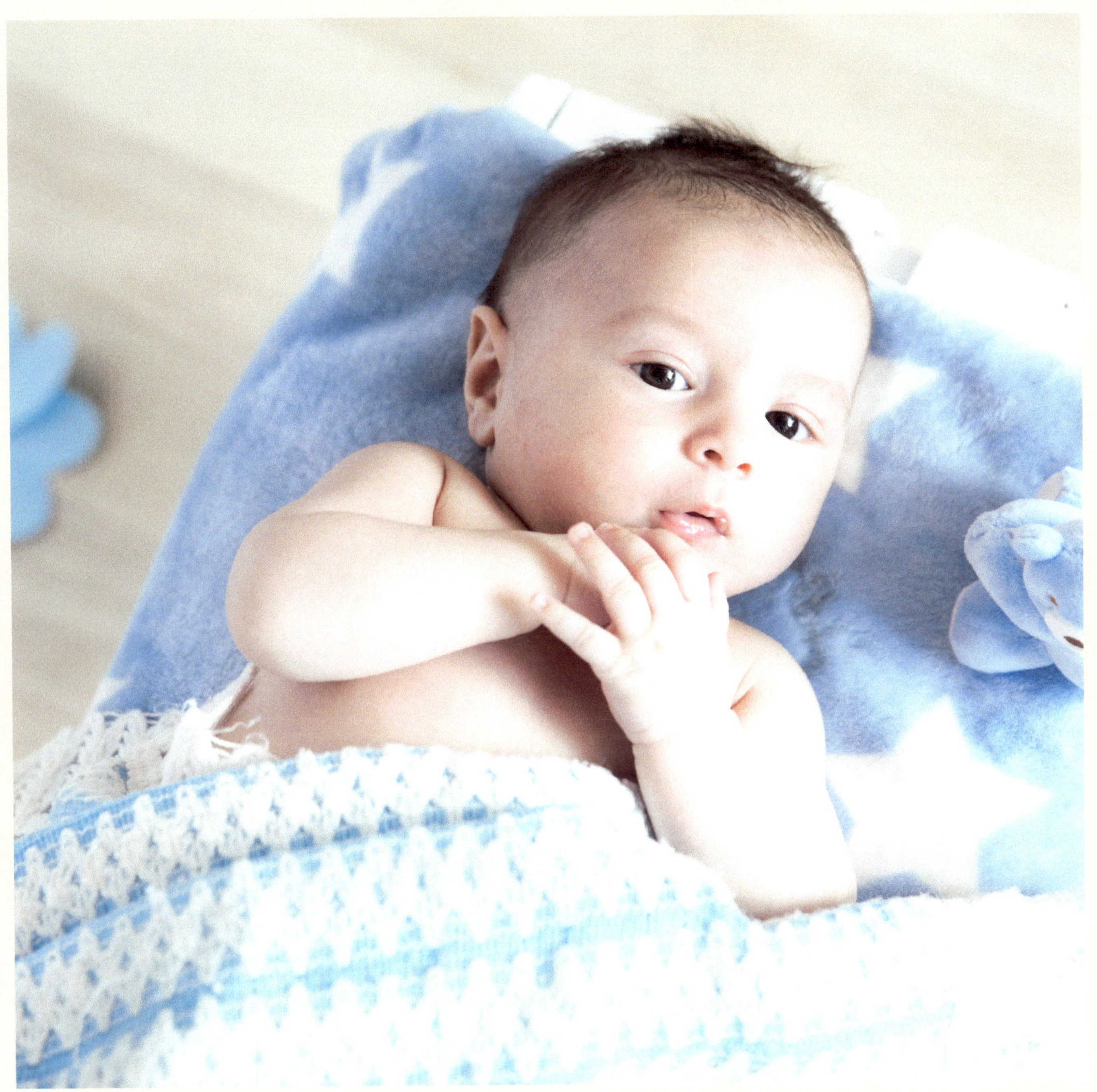

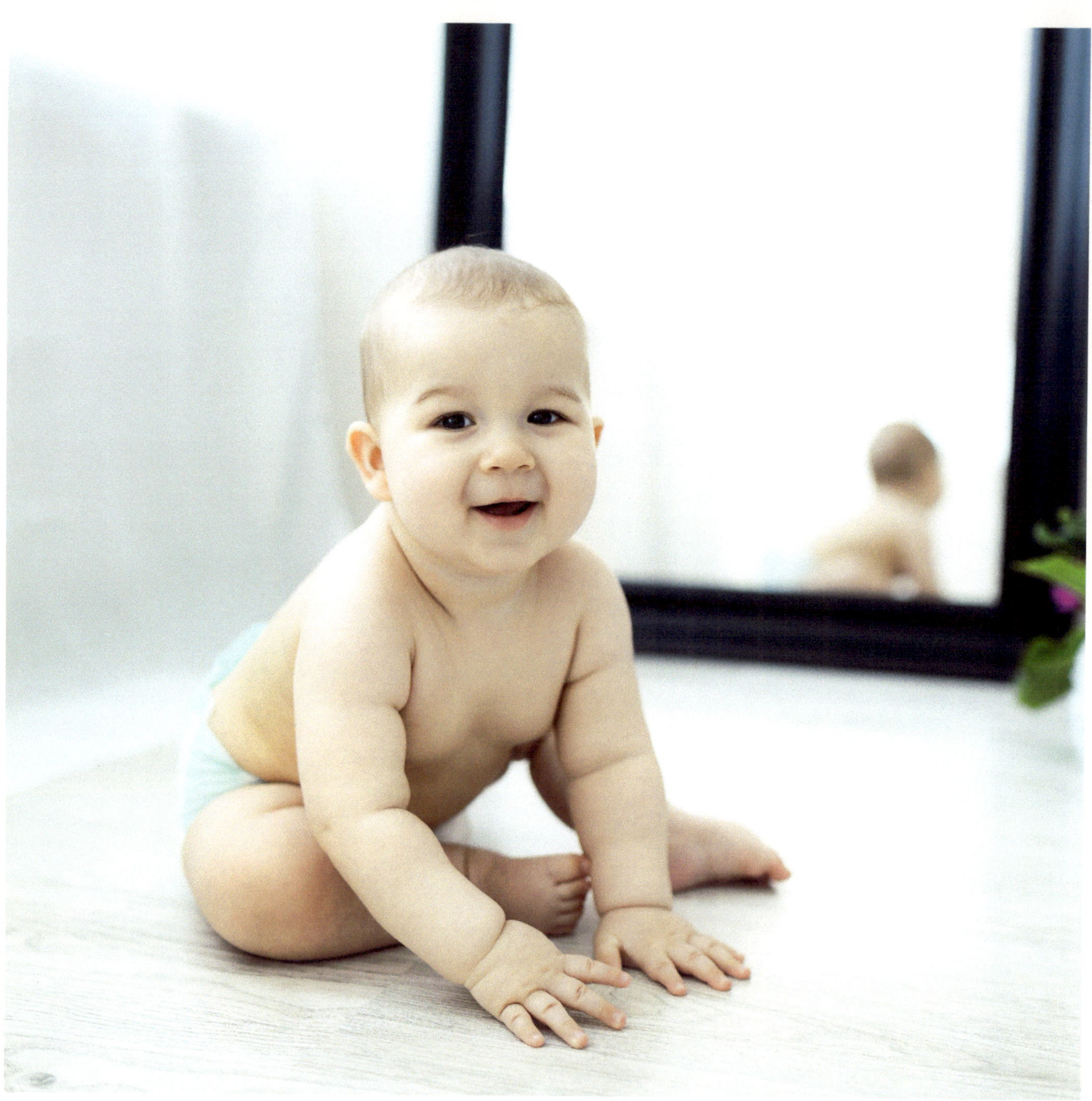

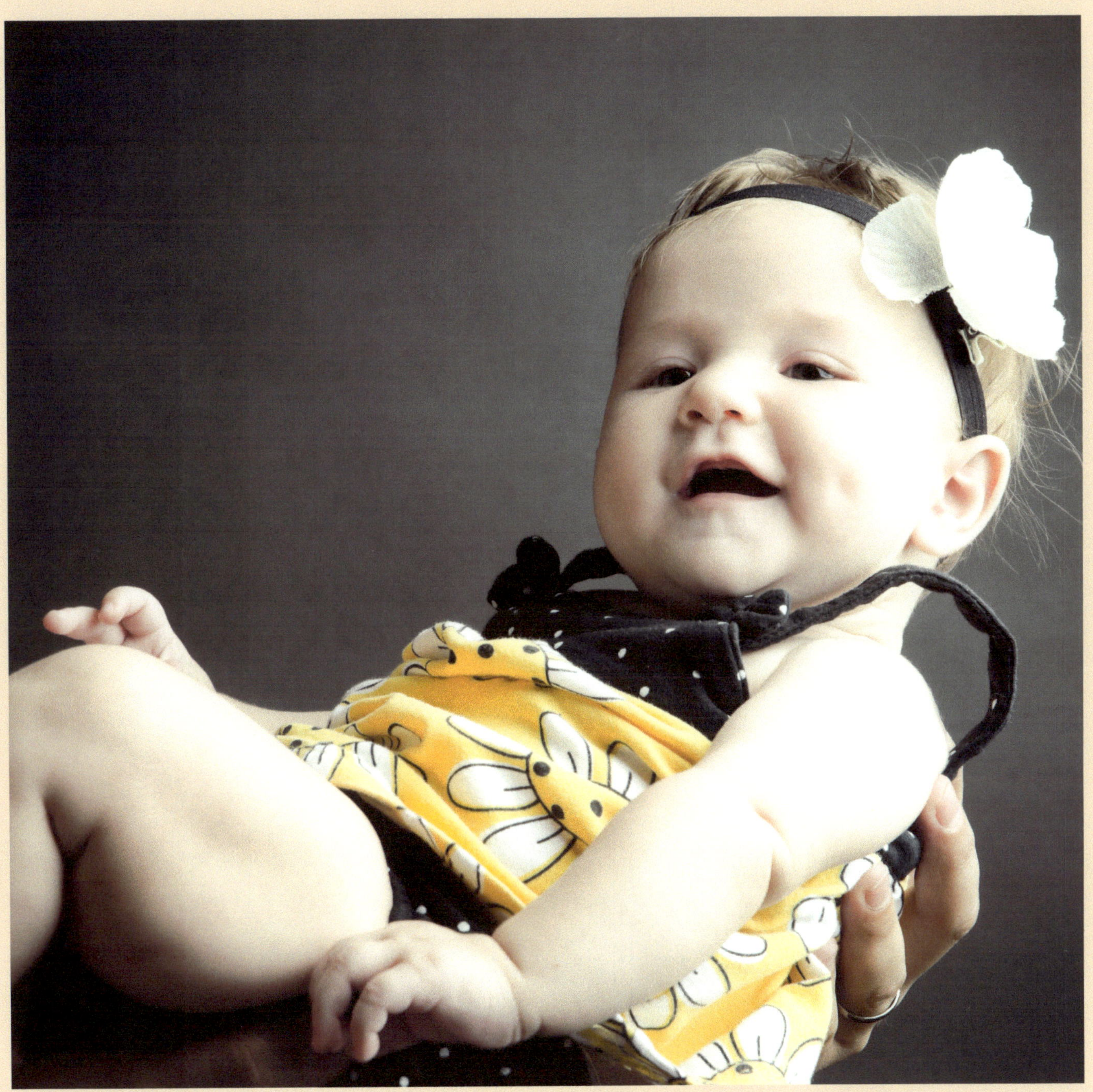

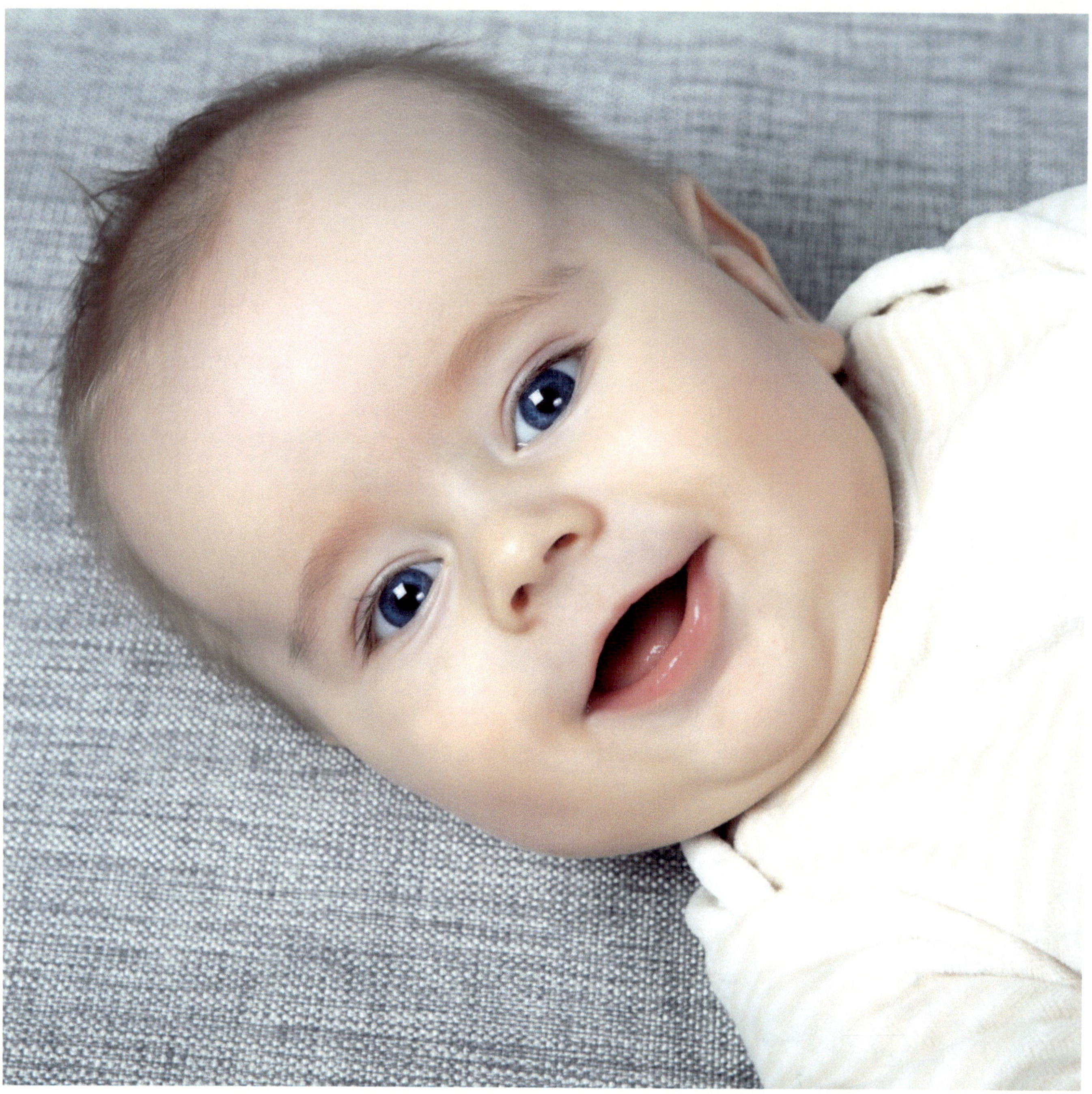

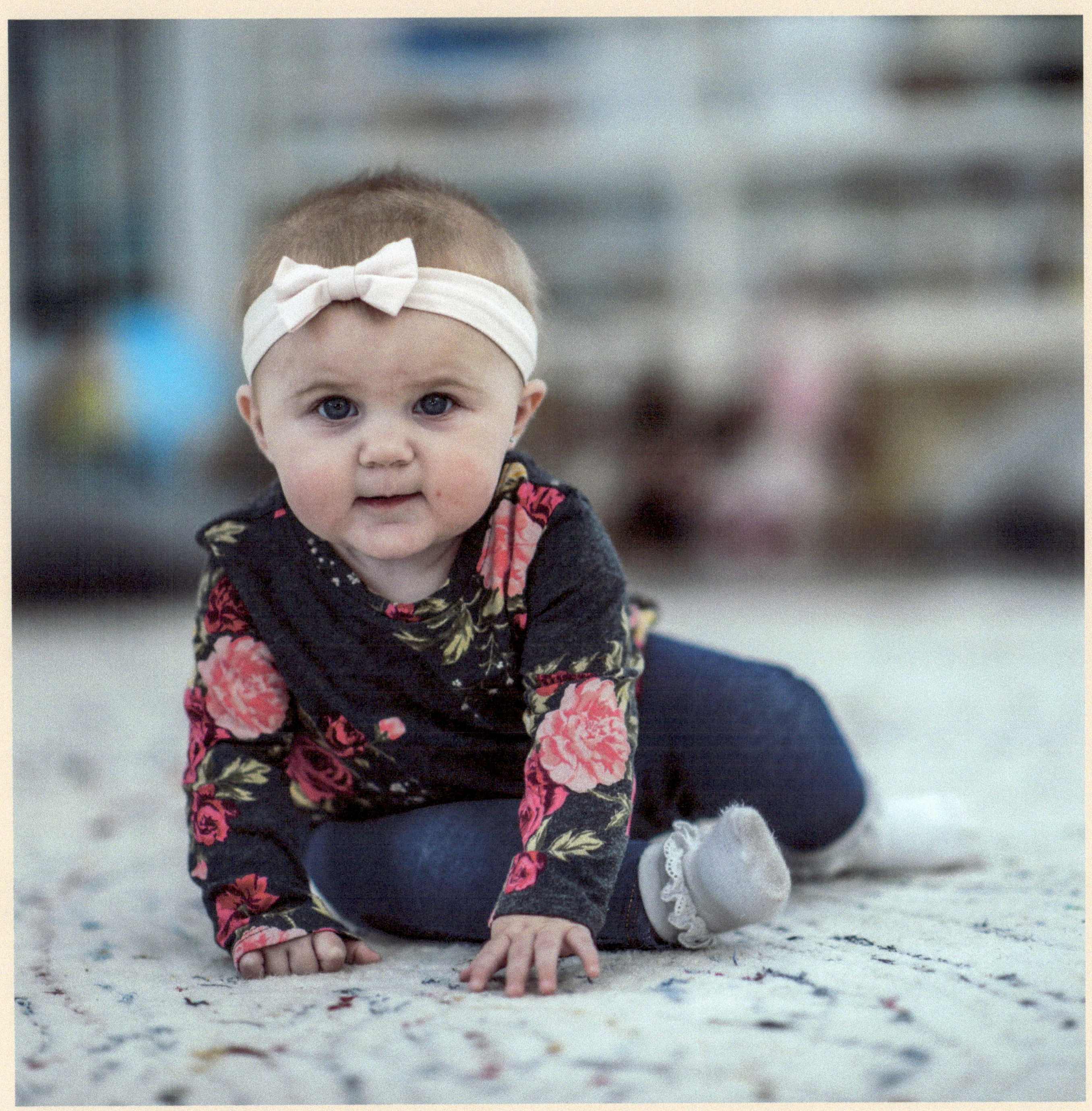

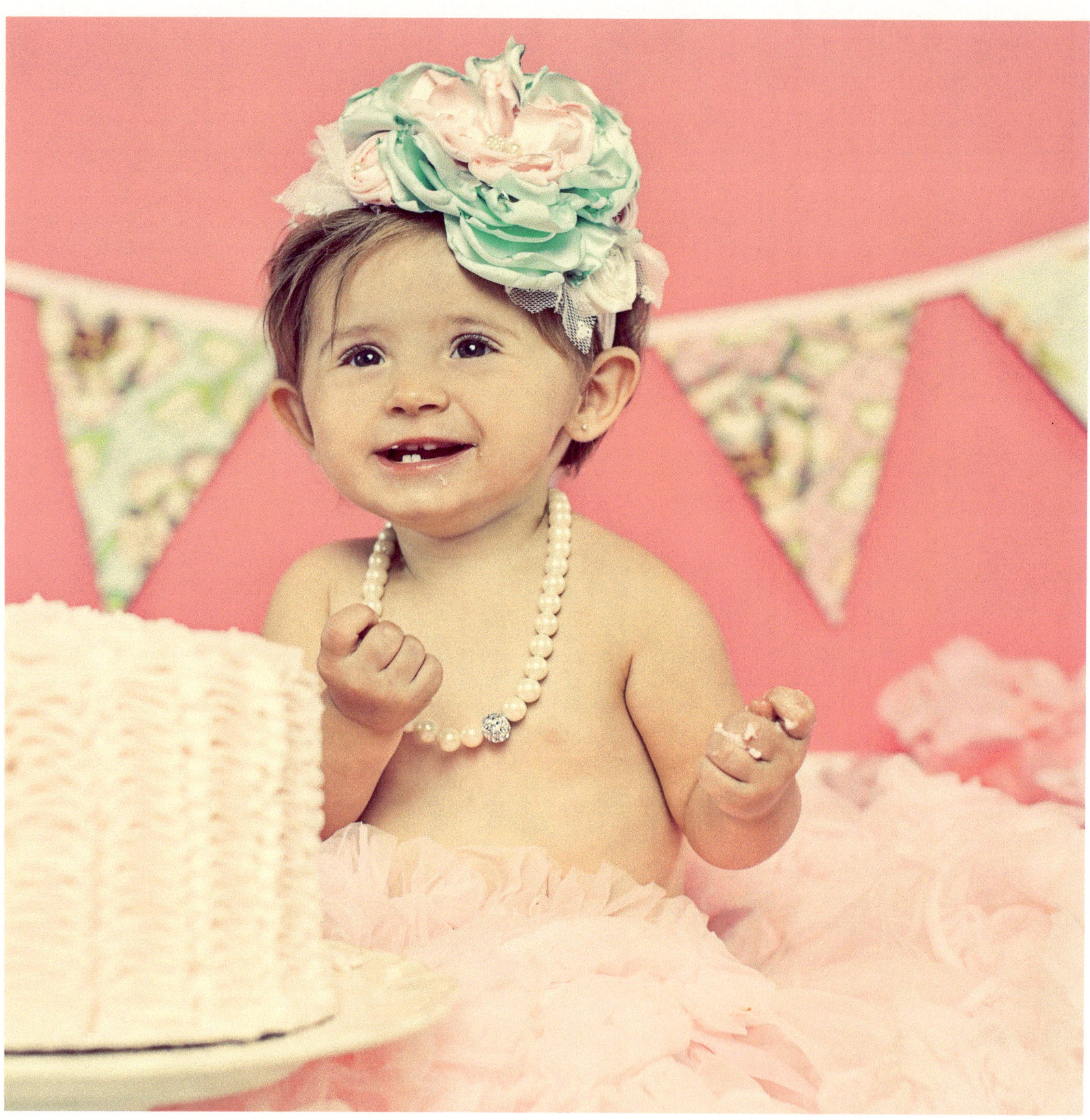

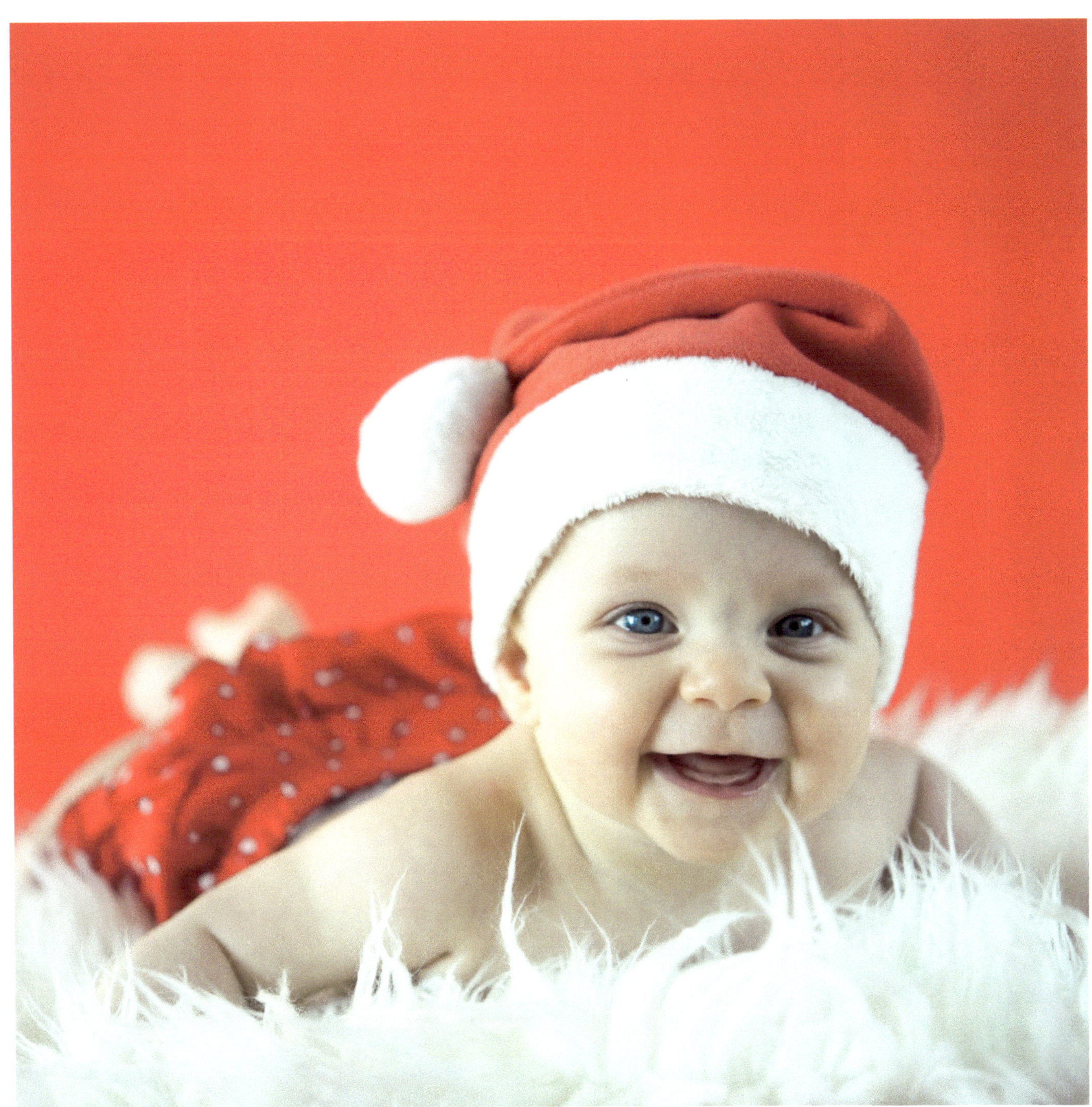

www.ingramcontent.com/pod-product-compliance
Ingram Content Group UK Ltd.
Pitfield, Milton Keynes, MK11 3LW, UK
UKHW060112300726
14090UKWH00002B/148

* 9 7 8 9 1 8 9 4 5 2 8 5 5 *